Grace So Amazing

Grace So Amazing

Dawn Smith Jordan

GSA Publishing
A Division of Jordan Ministries, Inc., Columbia, South Carolina

Grace So Amazing.

Copyright © 1993 by Dawn Smith Jordan.

Published by GSA Publishing
a division of Jordan Ministries, Inc.
Columbia, South Carolina.

Cover Photography: Ben Noey, Jr.

First printing 1993

Printed in the United States of America

Library of Congress Cataloging-in-Publication Data
Jordan, Dawn Smith.
    Grace so amazing / Dawn Smith Jordan.
        p.   cm.
    1. Jordan, Dawn Smith.   2. Contemporary Christian musicians—
United States—Biography.   I. Title
ML420.J776A3 1993   248.8'6'092—dc20   92-46888
ISBN 0-89107-699-9

01	00	99	98	97	96	95	94	93
15	14	13	12	11	10	9 8 7 6 5 4 3 2 1		

To my little brother
Robert
a precious part of my life.
We've both lost our sister,
but I thank God that we still have each other.
You are a gift of God's grace to me.
Your big sister is so proud of you
and loves you so very much.

Sharon (Shari) Faye Smith
June 25, 1967 - June 1, 1985

My Father's Plan

DAWN SMITH JORDAN and GARY DAVIS

My Father's way may twist and turn.
My heart may throb and ache,
but deep within my soul, I know
He never, ever makes mistakes.
There's so much now I cannot see.
My eyesight is far too dim,
but come what may, I'll simply trust,
and I will leave it all with Him.

CHORUS
I'm gonna trust in my Father's plan
even when I don't understand.
I need to cling to my Father's hand.
When I can't see
where He may lead—
still I will trust in my Father's plan.

And though the night may be dark,
and it seems day will never break,
I'll pin my faith, my all in Him
who makes not even one mistake.
My cherished plans may go astray,
my hopes, they all may fade away,
but still I'll trust in my Lord to lead,
for only He can know the way.

ACKNOWLEDGMENTS

THIS BOOK COULD NEVER HAVE BEEN WRITTEN WITHOUT THE help of many dear people. I offer sincere gratitude—

To my Lord and Savior, Jesus Christ, for Your infinite grace that is truly amazing.

To Jan and Lane Dennis for believing in my story, my book, and for welcoming me into the Crossway family.

To Lila Bishop for being such a wonderful editor and for making my book more readable.

To the staff of Crossway Books for your hard work and dedication to a job well done.

To my husband, Will, for your constant love to me, for walking with me through the difficult days of writing, for the many selfless hours spent reading and rereading my manuscript, for your help and suggestions, and for being such a precious evidence of God's grace in my life. I love you, Will.

In the editing process many names had to be left out of the final copy of this book. However, I will always be grateful for the love, sacrifice, help, and prayers of some who cannot go unmentioned. Eternal thanks and love to . . . Mom and Dad, Robert, Nana, Mom and Dad Jordan, Caroline, Britt, Page, Mema, Julie Caldwell, Cindy McDonald, Ken and Terry Pruitt, Uncle Louie and Aunt Barbara Lawrimore and family, Aunt

Sue Curran and family, Uncle Billy Cartrette, Uncle Ricky and Aunt Beverly Cartrette and family, the Lexington Baptist Church, the countless volunteers of Lexington County, Rev. Lewis Abbott, Johnny and Debbie Sorrell, Mike and Sherry Cates, Rev. Graham and Nancy Lyons, Rev. Ray Ridgeway, Mr. Gene Rountree, Mickey and Susan Wingard, Sally Yarber, Mark Heckle, Vonda and Kendra Hucks, Marge McGiboney, Jim and Cynthia Logan, Joe and Beverly Mack, Lanny and Sidney Palmer, the Miss Liberty Pageant Committee, the Miss South Carolina and Miss America Pageant, Joe, Gail, and Joey Sanders, Rita Allison, John Clark, Pete Petropoulos, Bob Pitts, Gerald and Linda Knight, Jim Leone, Jack Pollard, Tom Faircloth, Sherry Thrift Bradshaw, Dr. Billy Graham, Cliff Barrows, First Baptist Church of Columbia, Dr. Wendell Estep, Dr. John Bisagno, Kevin McAfee, Randy Smith, Gary Davis, Deputy Chief of Staff to the Governor of South Carolina Bob McAlister, Solicitor Donnie Myers and Knox McMahan, all witnesses and jury members who participated in the trial so sacrificially, and all the dear prayer warriors who supported me and my family through our tragedy. I will always be grateful to you all for your unforgettable touch upon my life. Forgive me if I have overlooked anyone.

I would like to pay special tribute to the countless law enforcement officers who gave sacrificially of their time and efforts on my family's case—in loving memory, Captain Leon Gasque of SLED; SLED Agents Ed Smith, Rick McCloud, and Paul Mirahn; former SLED Agent Lydia Glover; Lexington County Sheriff James Metts and Assistant Lewis McCarty; Captain Bob Ford; former Saluda County Sheriff George Booth, FBI Agent John Douglas; the Lexington County Sheriff's Department; the Lexington Police Department; the State

Highway Patrol; the South Carolina Law Enforcement Division; the Federal Bureau of Investigation, and the Emergency Preparedness Division of the Governor's Office of South Carolina. Words will never do enough to thank you, but my family and I will always be indebted to you.

And finally to you, the reader, thank you for taking time to ready my story. I pray that God will use it as a tool of ministry and encouragement in your life and that you too will find His grace truly sufficient (2 Corinthians 12:9). God bless you.

PREFACE

THIS IS A TRUE STORY—A STORY OF LIFE-SHATTERING TRAGEDY, but more than this, of God's unfailing grace. In the summer of 1985, the unthinkable happened to the Smiths, an All-American family of committed Christians. Their ordeal became the subject of a *Reader's Digest* feature story, the CBS made-for-television movie, *Nightmare in Columbia County,* and the PBS *New Explorers* program, "Profile in Terror."

Here now is the unreported side of this moving story, as lived and told by Dawn Smith (now Jordan)—how God has amazingly transformed this catastrophic experience into a ministry that has helped many people and has brought glory to His own name.

THE PUBLISHER

1

MAY 31, 1985, SEEMED LIKE ANY OTHER SPRING DAY IN CHAR-
lotte, NC—hot, already with the feel of summer. As Cindy and
I walked through the door of our apartment into the air-con-
ditioned coolness, I felt a sense of well-being. It was exciting
to be out on my own in my very first apartment, shared with
roommates Cindy and Jodie. I set down my squirming pack-
age, the hamster I'd bought for my sister Shari. I knew she'd
love this graduation gift.

Then I saw the look on Jodie's face.

"What's up? Something wrong?" I asked.

"Cindy, you need to call Dawn's mom," she said. "She
called while you guys were out and asked that you call as soon
as you got in."

Why in the world did my mom want Cindy to call her?
Cindy went into Jodie's bedroom and closed the door.

"Jodie, has something happened?" I asked nervously.
"Jodie, tell me. I have a right to know what's going on."

"All I know," she began, "is that your mom told me that
Shari has been abducted, and I don't exactly know what that
means."

I knew what it meant, but it didn't register in my mind. I

15

barged into the room where Cindy was and demanded that she give me the phone.

"Mom, what's going on?" I asked.

"Dawn, Shari's missing and you need to come home immediately."

What? Surely there was some mistake. Shari had probably gone shopping with her friends and forgotten to tell Mom and Dad. With the excitement of her senior cruise to the Bahamas, anything was possible. Or she could have been with her boyfriend, Richard. No need to jump to conclusions. And as my mother began to tell me bits and pieces of what had happened, I couldn't believe what I was hearing.

"Mom, I can't come home. I've got to be here to perform tomorrow."

"Dawn, we will talk about that later, but right now you just need to pack, and a patrolman will pick you up in a few minutes," she said sternly.

This was too much for me to handle. A patrolman? "Can Cindy come with me?" I asked foolishly, not wanting to make the trip alone.

"No, Dawn, we don't know how long you'll be here," Mom said.

I broke into tears in the middle of the den, while Cindy headed to the bedroom to pack my things. Just then a friend of ours, Kimbol, came in the front door. He was just stopping by to say hi, but his usual jovial expression changed abruptly when he saw the fear written all over my face.

"What's wrong, baby? What is it?"

That was all it took. I crumpled to the floor, sobbing helplessly. As he picked me up to calm me, Cindy explained what had happened. He knew Shari well, since the three of us were performers in the shows at Carowinds Theme Park.

The phone rang again. It was Dad telling Cindy when the policeman would arrive for me. "Cindy," he said matter-of-factly, "we feel maybe it would be best if you follow behind the patrol car so Dawn can have someone here she's close to."

Blurred thoughts darted in and out of my mind as I rode in the patrol car, Cindy following in her little orange Volvo. The two-hour drive from Charlotte to Lexington, SC, seemed endless although we must have been going at least eighty. I began to pray. It was the only thing I knew to do. *Oh, God, what is ahead of me once this trip comes to an end? I'm so scared of what I may find. Please, God, please let it be some mistake. Please let Shari be okay.*

But when we pulled into our driveway, the crowd of people and police cars told me there had been no mistake.

"Dear Jesus," I whispered.

I made my way up the familiar brick steps and into the house, and I finally caught sight of my mother's face in the crowd of friends, family members, and officers. The fear I'd heard in her voice over the phone was in her eyes. I wanted to shout, *I'm sorry. I shouldn't have thought of myself or the stupid show at a time like this, but this was so unreal to me there, a hundred miles away.* Now it was only too real, and I couldn't handle it.

The police, deputies, and people with the State Law Enforcement Division (SLED) began questioning my family and me immediately. I was overwhelmed by the things they were asking. Did I think it was possible that Shari could have run away? Did I know of anyone who might have taken her for any reason?

As always in a situation like this, there were rumors.

People had reported seeing a girl of Shari's description getting into a red sports car with a young, dark-haired man. Others reported seeing a young woman being forced into a car, and the list went on.

Up in my bedroom after the questioning had finally stopped for a while, I went back over everything in my mind again. I couldn't believe that Shari ran away. We'd been raised in a very strict household, to the point of being afraid of our father. He lived out the proverb, "Spare the rod, spoil the child." As most children do, we'd talked about running away before—after being punished. Shari had threatened to carry it out; she'd called me in tears a few times when I was away at Columbia College, asking if she could come and stay with me, but I knew she wasn't serious. She loved our family too much to hurt us like this.

I refused to give in to my worst fears. Shari was going to be all right, and I determined to pray harder than I ever had in my life. Didn't the Bible say that anything we asked in Jesus' name we'd receive? I knew God wouldn't let anything horrible happen—would He?

2

AS THE SUN BEGAN TO SET AND DARKNESS CAME, I KEPT THINK-
ing, *Surely this isn't happening to my family. This is the kind of
thing you only read about in the paper.* Wasn't Shari going to
wheel into the driveway any minute in her little blue Chevette,
pop in the front door, and tell us all about her high school
graduation rehearsal and the party she and her friends had
had that afternoon? No, she couldn't. Her car had been found
running, with the door open and her purse inside, right where
she'd left it when she went to the mailbox.

Dad had looked out the front window around 3:30 P.M. and
said to Mom, "Shari's home." Then minutes later he realized
she'd still not made it to the house. Fear had gripped him as
he grabbed his car keys and headed up the 750-foot driveway.
He found the car empty and no sign of Shari.

Back in the house, he met Mom in the foyer.

"Honey," he said, "I don't know where Shari is, but she's
gone."

"No, Bob," Mom said fearfully. "Not Shari—not my
Shari."

They held each other's shaking hands and prayed together
for their daughter's safety, claiming the verse they'd always
turned to when anything went wrong, Romans 8:28: "All

things work together for good to those who love the Lord, and are called according to His purpose." Dad told Mom to call the sheriff, and he went out to look for his daughter.

Shortly, the sheriff, his deputies, and volunteers began to search the wooded area near our home. Friends and people we didn't even know turned up to help in the search, as well as police, bloodhounds, two airplanes, and two sheriff's department helicopters, using their powerful floodlights. They found footprints leading from the car to the mailbox, but no return tracks. Shari had been barefoot and was probably wearing her swimsuit at the time of her disappearance. The State Law Enforcement Division joined in and alerted authorities statewide of the suspected abduction.

My brother Robert, then fifteen, had gone to play golf with some of his buddies at the Lexington Country Club. Someone heard about what had happened and found him out on the course. Soon after that, he walked through the front door, dirty-faced from the heat. As always, he tried to be strong for Mom, but he was frightened, as we all were.

Family members and friends began to come, to help in any way they could with food, prayers, and support. My best friend and college roommate, Julie, had been baby-sitting when a friend called to tell her what had happened, and she was there as soon as she heard. By this point, there was tight security at the entrance of our driveway, but they knew that Julie was on her way and let her in with no questions.

Having people there who loved us kept us from falling completely apart. As we all gathered into the living room, our hands naturally joined, and people began to pray . . . for Shari's safety, for us, and for the searchers and local authorities. None of us could hold back the tears. God's presence was strong in that crowded room. When we sang "Amazing Grace," the song I'd grown up singing all those years in church, I knew that same grace was somehow with us in that moment.

Julie, Cindy, and I made our way upstairs and stopped at the bathroom window, dazed by the horror of lights, trucks, and unbelievable confusion on the front lawn.

"Dawn, we're never going to be the same again," Cindy said in a voice I'd never heard her use before.

I could hardly respond as I walked toward my bedroom. All I cared about was getting Shari back from wherever she was. Little did I know then how true Cindy's statement would prove to be.

By 10:30 we were getting more worried. The search party found Shari's red bandana one-half mile down the road from our home. There were no other clues at this point, and darkness finally called the search to a halt. They had no evidence that this was a kidnapping, but it was the only logical conclusion.

The sheriff of Lexington County, James Metts, had received reports of two suspicious vehicles in the area, but no evidence to link the cars to Shari's disappearance. One of the vehicles, a late-model yellow Chevrolet Monte Carlo, had been driven by a dark-haired, bearded man who was being sought for questioning.

The police were still questioning us to see if we could possibly think of anything else that would help them. Waiting was agonizing. As the minutes of that first night dragged on, fearful thoughts filled our minds. *Who had Shari? Would he hurt her? What was she feeling?* We had little hope of sleeping that night, but we were finally persuaded to try. So we lay down fully dressed—Mom, Dad, Robert, and I—all on their king-size bed, restlessly waiting to find out where the other precious member of our family was.

●

The sound of a helicopter flying overhead jerked me awake. I wearily made my way to the glass front door and looked out. Our front yard and pasture had been taken over by an army of some sort. Fear gnawed in the pit of my stomach. It was only 6:00 A.M., and already a helicopter was parked in the middle of the field with a crowd of at least 250 volunteers. I felt so helpless just waiting inside when so many people were out there doing their best to help us—searching for . . . what? Sickening thoughts raced through my head. I wondered how Mom and Dad were handling this.

By now we had another worry. Shari suffered from a rare disease called diabetes insipidus, commonly known as "water diabetes." There were only a few cases of the illness in South Carolina. It could be controlled with a prescribed "miracle drug" in the form of a nasal spray. One container was always kept in my parents' refrigerator and another in Shari's purse, which had been left in her car. Without the medication, she would need three to four liters of water every hour to keep from severely dehydrating. Without enough water or the medicine, she could pass out and become comatose within two days. The situation had reached "critical proportions," as Captain Bob Ford of the Lexington County Sheriff's Department put it in a news release.

It was some time during the morning that Lydia Glover with SLED asked me if she and I could go up into my room and talk. She patiently waited as I emotionally began to tell her things I thought would help. She asked if Shari might have run away. I didn't think so. Shari and another student had been chosen to sing the national anthem as a duet at her graduation ceremony the next day, and then she was going on a cruise. Around noon yesterday Shari had called Mom and asked to meet her at the bank to get her traveler's checks for the trip. As they stood before the teller, Mom was thinking how cute Shari looked in her white baggy shorts, pullover shirt, and baby doll socks and shoes. Shari had hugged Mom extra tightly and thanked her again for letting her go on the cruise. She was on top of the world.

Lydia asked about our family life. I explained that ours was your basic, all-American, middle class family. Our home was always busy, with people running here and there—along with dogs, cats, gerbils, horses, and a stray bird once in a while—trying to make our hectic and oftentimes crazy schedules work together. Dad was hard-working and a good provider. Although we were never wealthy, we always had what we needed and lived comfortably. Mom was a homemaker, but she would work part time substitute teaching at the schools we attended. She said she did it just to keep up with us. We were proud that our friends could meet our "cool" and pretty mom. But she was first a full-time wife and mother— always there to welcome us home at the end of those long school days, to listen to each of us tell our news of the day. Robert, Shari, and I had a lot of fun growing up together, and we were taught to love and cherish our family as God intended.

Some of Lydia's questions were so hard to think about, much less answer. No, there had never been any sexual abuse, etc., etc. I tried to explain the best I knew how what it had been like growing up in our home. I was very grateful to have two parents who loved their children and raised them on Biblical principles. Every morning after breakfast, we all sat around the kitchen table for family devotions before we left for school. We would hold hands and pray before we went our separate ways. Sometimes it was impossible for three mischievous children to sit quietly, and we'd either be pinching, squeezing, or giggling. And sometimes due to oversleeping, lost sox, etc., we missed the time altogether. But our parents put their best effort into establishing the importance of a time with God before each day began. It was there I learned to spend time with the Lord in His Word and prayer on my own—a practice which would later become the vital source of strength in my life.

We'd been faithful church members as far back as I could remember. Mom and Dad had encouraged me when I accepted Jesus as my personal Savior at the age of nine. I was so excited on the night I was to be baptized. I was ready to begin my new life as a Christian. Shari followed by choosing to give her life to Jesus a few years later, and then Robert. My parents were thrilled as each of their children made this most important of life's decisions.

We'd had happy times as well as hard times. Dad was a disciplinarian and made no excuses for it. Although at times we felt his discipline was too firm and overbearing, I am grateful for the way the Lord used him to instill in me a respect for authority and a desire to do what's right. There was never a question in our home concerning basic moral issues, and I believe that knowledge saved us from many problems. We had enough fear in our hearts to make sure we did our best to obey our parents. Proverbs 22:6 was true of my life: "Train up a child in the way he should go; even when he is old he will not depart from it." It was a strict household to grow up in, but Mom and Dad always said they had our best interests in mind, and I believe they did.

●

As the day wore on, I wandered through the rooms of the house and at one point went to Dad's office to check on him and Mom. This small office at the east side of the house where Dad worked as a salesman of electronic scoreboards and signs was the one place in the house where they could just be alone.

Dad looked up at me from his chair, the trauma showing in his face. "If Shari ran away," he said, "she did it because she couldn't stand having to measure up to you any longer. Bless her heart, she always felt like she was being compared to you, always feeling second."

Anger welled up inside of me. I so wanted to tell him just what I thought might be the reason for Shari running away, but that old fear of him took over. His words hurt me deeply. The hot tears I tried to suppress stung my face. If the truth were known, Shari was a much better singer than I was. She just had a natural talent for singing with everything she had. But she had always felt she had to compete with me, and I hated it. I know she was proud that I had won singing competitions and had a performing job at Carowinds, but she compared herself with me unfavorably, as younger sisters often tend to do.

Shari had had some hard breaks with her singing. Soon after being hired at Carowinds to sing and dance in the country show, she found out that she had nodules on her vocal cords. She had to quit the show and remain quiet for six weeks at the doctor's orders. It had been hard on all of us, and I hated to see my sister go through such a heartbreaking disappointment. It was unusual for a seventeen-year-old to make it into the cast, and she wanted to do her best. She would come home after the weekend rehearsals at Carowinds and spend literally hours on the paved part of the driveway under the basketball goal, singing and vigorously practicing the clogging routines. She'd call me up excitedly and have me listen to the tape of the show over the phone. She was a born performer.

After the doctors ordered her to stop using her voice, she would get in her little car and turn up her radio and tapes and sing as loudly as she could, so her boyfriend Richard informed me. I knew my sister well enough to know that she just couldn't stand not to sing. Richard said he would tell her to stop, but she wouldn't even hear him. To try to encourage her while I was away at school, I would call her and just talk to her. She was to tap once on the receiver for yes and twice for no. But Shari could not stand this ridiculous way of communicating, and she would eventually tell me that she thought this was stupid and hang up. She had a mind of her own.

My mind drifted back to the first time Shari had sung a solo in church. She was so little the minister of music had to get her a box to stand on so the congregation could see her over the rostrum. But there was definitely nothing small about her voice. She stood up there confidently in front of that whole congregation and belted it out, loving every minute of it. Soon after that, we were asked to sing in church together. We'd spend hour after hour arguing over who would sing what part, but when we got in front of the church, we smiled like little angels! Mom, Dad, and Robert knew the truth, however.

Music had played a large part in our lives as we were growing up. Mom and Dad both played the piano and sang, and Dad had also taught himself to play the guitar, dulcimer, and trumpet. Shari and I took piano lessons, and Robert was learning the guitar. However, it was singing that Shari and I loved. Dad had bought us a tape recorder, and we'd practice hour after hour on duets, recording our songs, and then listening to see how we sounded. Soon we were ready for concerts. Using hairbrushes or hair dryers for microphones, a garbage can turned upside down for Robert's drum, and a flashlight for our spotlight, we performed for our audience— Dad, Mom, and occasionally our grandparents. We'd coax Robert into singing with us every now and then, but he preferred munching on Doritos during the performance. His favorite song, and practically the only one we could get him to sing, was "People to People," which he warbled sweetly in his little soprano voice.

Shari and I became known as the "Smith Sisters" in the area, and churches began to ask us to come and sing for their services and revivals. We would go with Dad when he ministered in prisons and at a boys' correctional school, and we'd sing before he spoke. We sang in local nursing homes and just about anywhere we were invited. Once we even sang at a furniture store grand opening. They had real posters with our names and pictures on them, and we thought we'd made it big! Dad had bought us a portable sound system that was constantly set up in the living room for our hours of rehearsal. He had even talked with a Nashville agent at one time who said he thought we had talent. Talk of our going to Nashville and cutting a record thrilled us!

Those memories were so precious to me. As my thoughts turned back to the present reality, I began to realize that the times of singing with my sister could be gone forever. *Oh, God, please don't let that be,* I pleaded.

3

ALL THROUGH THAT LONG SATURDAY, UNBELIEVABLE THINGS went on outside the doors of our home, which made us even more afraid of what could be happening somewhere else. A tractor-trailer from the Emergency Preparedness Division of the Governor's Office, equipped with radios and a telephone, was set up in the front yard as a command post. Everything happened with an obvious urgency that only increased my fear. A local business set up a tent, and friends sent sandwiches, potato chips, cases of soft drinks, and ice for the searchers. Our front field looked like some sort of carnival!

Early in the day the phone rang. Our worst fears seemed to be confirmed as the caller told us he had kidnapped Shari and demanded a ransom. But later it turned out to be a hoax. It made me realize that while many kind, concerned people really wanted to help, there were also those who were cruel beyond my understanding. How could someone do such a hateful thing to my family at a time like this?

All throughout the day the ground search continued. Two people fainted from heat exhaustion, one man stepped on a nail, and an officer suffered a spider bite. All four were taken by ambulance, which stood by most of the day, to Lexington County Hospital.

By 5:00 P.M., the sheriff sent the civilian searchers home to get some rest, as the temperature hovered at 97 degrees. Most had been out since dawn and had covered more than twenty miles on foot. They were told to return to resume the search the next morning at 7:30.

It was hard to believe that a whole day had passed, a day that seemed like eternity, without finding Shari. When evening came, my mother and father went out into the night to get some fresh air. Mom, so desperate for some hope that her daughter would be all right, said that as she looked up into the heavens, she saw one star glimmer much brighter than all the rest and knew somehow that it was a sign from God that Shari was all right. How we all wanted to believe it.

My aunt Barbara, who had arrived earlier that day along with my grandmother, "Nana," and other family members, was sitting in the living room when Mom came in with her hopeful news. My aunt said, with a most determined look on her face, "Shari's alive, and I know it for a fact. She's going to be just fine."

That was exactly what we all wanted to hear.

The night dragged on as police continued to follow the various leads called in. We had the graduation ceremony tomorrow in the back of our minds, and we prayed that Shari would make it home safely before the day came.

But Sunday morning, June 2, arrived with no news. As the time for the graduation ceremony drew near, with a twinge of pain I remembered Peachy, the hamster I had bought for my sister. He was now in Jodie's care. I still had Shari's graduation card in my suitcase, with a message already written on it, telling her how very proud her big sister was of her and that I couldn't wait for her to be at college with me in the fall. I would have given anything to be able to hand her that card right then.

But guilt and regret also nagged at my conscience that morning. Earlier in the week a very odd thing had happened to me. Two nights before Shari's disappearance, I had awakened in tears with the strangest feeling that something was wrong with Shari or that something was going to happen to her. Was it a premonition? I'd never experienced anything like it before. I woke Cindy up and told her about it.

"Dawn, you've just had a bad dream. Don't worry about it. Try to go back to sleep."

"I can't. It's too real."

"Listen, Dawn, if you still feel the same way in the morning, you can call your parents. But don't wake them up now. You need to get some sleep."

I tried to take her advice and finally fell asleep. But when I awoke, the fear that had swept over me in the night hadn't gone away. Although I couldn't dismiss it, I didn't mention it to my parents either. How I wish I had! If only I had said something, Mom and Dad might have told Shari to be more careful, or Shari might have been more suspicious. But, on the other hand, maybe she would have just laughed it off.

●

The continuing search cast a pall of doom over the high school graduation. Many Lexington High School students wanted to postpone it. However, at my parents' request, the ceremony went on as planned. At the beginning of the exercises, Principal Carl Fulmer acknowledged the anxiety so close to the surface in the auditorium. "We're touched by the absence of one of our classmates. Shari Smith's family knows how much every one of us cares for them in their time of need. At their request, we are going on with this ceremony." Several of her fellow chorus members and friends wept during a brief silent prayer in her honor and as the national anthem was sung by Andy Aun, who had been scheduled to sing it with Shari. During the ceremony, an empty chair in the second row reminded graduates of their missing classmate.

It was all so unfair! How could something like this happen to Shari? She had everything going for her. She was beautiful, talented, popular—the only one in her senior class who had won two awards, Most Talented and the Wittiest. Because only one award was allowed per person, the Most Talented was given to another girl. Shari was choir vice-president and vocalist for the school's jazz band. Her chorus teacher described her as "the most talented student I ever taught."

As the unfruitful search continued through that day, an estimated three hundred to five hundred volunteers, some from other counties, helped law enforcement officers. Sheriff Metts went out to the reporters who constantly flocked at the entrance to our property. "In all my years of law enforcement, I've never seen the turnout of people in support of something like this," he told them.

Again and again during the day, Dad and the people from the sheriff's department and SLED withdrew behind closed doors for conferences. I kept staring at the door, wondering what was going on there, praying for wisdom for them.

When the day came to a close, I realized I was dreading the night. For some reason, the darkness brought all my fears to the surface. My parents had taught us as children that the dark was nothing to be afraid of, and I knew that, but that didn't help the gnawing in my stomach. The first two nights had been so dreadful, I didn't think I could face another one. I wondered how much longer this could possibly go on.

Exhausted from lack of sleep and the unbearable stress, our family was finally convinced to try to get some rest. Once again, all four of us were in my parents' room.

●

I must have been dozing because when the phone rang, it startled me. I glanced at the clock on the nightstand and saw it was around 2:20 A.M. Dad answered it, and the caller wanted to speak to Mom. She wearily made her way to the phone on the other nightstand, dazed from the mild sedative she had been given. The male voice on the other end was matter-of-fact. He asked if it was Mrs. Smith and then if she was all right and awake. He said that, so she would know it was not a hoax, he was going to tell her certain things concerning Shari.

As she clumsily waved her hands for something to write on, Dad fumbled through the bedside drawers to find a pencil and paper. Mom began jotting down notes. The male voice said that we'd receive in the mail that day around one or two o'clock a letter from Shari. He told Mom what the letter would look like, saying that at the top would be written 6/1/85, 3:10 A.M.

I heard Mom ask, "Who is this?"

The man described the clothes Shari had on at the time of her disappearance—a black and yellow bathing suit, white baggy shorts, and a yellow shirt worn over her swimsuit. He even said that Shari was aware that her daddy might be upset about the new suit. Then abruptly he said, "You are looking in the wrong direction. Have Sheriff Metts get on the TV at 7:00 A.M. on Channel 10 and call off the search. Please call off the search. They are wasting time at this location."

Mom asked two or three more times who the caller was, and then he hung up. She placed the receiver down with a confused look on her face. "That was him. He has Shari, and I didn't even realize it at first. He sounded so clear. I just thought he was someone with the sheriff's department until he began talking so strangely about the search being in the wrong place and describing exactly what Shari was wearing."

Immediately, Sheriff Metts, Lewis McCarty, and Captain Leon Gasque with SLED were in the room going over Mom's notes. There was no mention of ransom or anything else to make sense out of the situation. Mom didn't recognize the voice of the caller. But now we knew for sure. Shari had been kidnapped.

The caller had stayed on the phone long enough for the call to be traced. It had been made from Taylor's Store on Highway 378 just outside of Lexington; however, by the time the authorities arrived, they found no one. They dusted the phone booth for prints, but found none. Although no one knew if he'd call again, the sheriff's department and SLED agents immediately hooked a recording device up to our phone.

It terrified us to think that some stranger could have Shari somewhere in that dark night. Once again, I found myself praying desperately that God would somehow spare my precious sister's life. I couldn't imagine the awful fear she must be experiencing. My older-sister instinct took over, and I wanted to bear her terror myself instead. I knew Shari was brave and very strong-willed, but none of us had ever been prepared for anything like this.

I found it impossible to sleep the rest of that Sunday night. My emotions were shattered. We were living the most horrible nightmare imaginable. When would it end? And how?

BECAUSE THE PRESS COVERAGE WAS SO MASSIVE, THE CALL WAS kept confidential—to stop any more rumors from spreading and to ease the panic of other parents and residents in the area. The people of Lexington County were scared, and they seemed to be making up their own stories. Rumors circulated that Shari was dead, among other things, as people "on the outside" speculated on news passing along the grapevine that had grown up over the last three days.

It was Monday, June 3. The volunteer search had been called off the day before, and my parents had gone out to the end of the driveway to personally thank all the hundreds of people that had helped so sacrificially.

A specially equipped plane provided by the FBI would be flown in from Washington, DC, to aid the authorities as they continued to look for Shari. The plane's infrared sensors would be able to cover a wider area than the volunteers had. I knew infrared sensors were used to search for bodies. I couldn't stand the thought of that plane being successful in its mission. I wanted to believe that Shari was alive, but it had been so long since her last dose of medicine. I knew she was in serious trouble by then.

I remembered when Shari was around four years old, my

parents had taken her to the hospital for the tests which finally brought the diagnosis of diabetes insipidus. She lay in her bed with tubes and IVs coming out of her frail little body. Because of the disease and tests, the doctors had to hold back any water from her for hours at a time while she cried and begged my mother for a drink. Watching her suffer was heartbreaking for my parents. Finally she would become so dehydrated that when the skin on her small arm was pinched, it would stay in that pinched position afterward. Then, when it seemed she could stand no more, the doctors would allow her to drink again. It was a long, trying process, but necessary in order to find medications to help her live as normal a life as possible. I could only pray that Shari was not lying somewhere now, dehydrated and crying for help.

The hours dragged on. I would find myself continually looking at the clock to see how much time had elapsed since the last time I'd checked. I had to make myself think what day it was. It was only Monday? I couldn't believe Shari had been gone for three whole days. It seemed as if those three days were my whole life. I could hardly remember what life had been like before this had happened. As I once again glanced at the clock, I saw that it was a little after 3:00 in the afternoon.

Suddenly my thoughts were interrupted by the sound of the telephone ringing, and I knew what I had to do. There was no way of knowing who was going to be on the other end of the line, but it was my job to answer it. I was to try to keep the man on the phone as long as I possibly could. There might be some chance that the kidnapper would now turn his attention to me. Rumors that the kidnapper had actually been after me were going around—that he had mistakenly gotten Shari. At this point, we had no idea.

"Hello?" I answered, as calmly as I could.

"Mrs. Smith?" came a male voice on the other end, sounding somewhat distorted.

"No. This is Dawn."

"I need to speak to your mother," he said.

Doing as I had been coached, I asked, "Can I ask who's calling?"

"No."

That was it—such a short answer. "Okay. Okay, hold on a second, please," I replied.

When my mother picked up the phone, he immediately asked her if we'd received the mail that day. She told him yes.

"Do you believe me now?" His voice sounded muffled, as if he were trying to disguise it.

"Well, I'm not sure I believe you because I haven't had any word from Shari, and I need to know that she is well," my mother said, her voice almost choking with fear and emotion.

"You'll know in two or three days," was his short reply.

"Why two or three days?" The panic now sounded in her voice.

"Call off the search," he said unemotionally.

"Tell me if she is well because of her disease. Are you taking care of her?" Mom pleaded, but there was no answer. He had already hung up.

My heart went out to my mother. We were all torn up, but in that instant I felt her pain was much deeper than ours. She and Shari were so close, and I couldn't bear to think what it would do to her if anything happened . . .

What had been the purpose of that phone call? Again, no ransom had been mentioned. We were no better off than before—simply more worried. The call was traced to a phone

booth just outside of Eckerd's at the Town Square Shopping
Center off Highway 1 in Lexington. Again no one was there
when the authorities arrived.

One ray of hope—we had taped the conversation. As we
listened again and again to the recording, it was obvious to us
that this person was using some type of electronic device to
alter his voice. But that was all we knew.

I remembered the long talk Lydia and I had had upstairs
in my bedroom with the door closed. She showed me a composite drawing of a suspect that various people had seen, and
she had asked me to give her the names of any men I thought
capable of kidnapping Shari. I began to suspect everyone.
Shari was so beautiful; plenty of guys at school wanted to date
her, and she didn't give the time of day to some of them. She
had worked at the flea market concession stand right down
the road from our home part time, and there was no way of
knowing who might have seen her there. Lydia had also
wanted to know about people at church.

Suddenly, fear swept through me. The person could be
someone I or my family knew well. I was suspecting everyone,
and I couldn't believe it. We listened to the tape repeatedly to
make sure we didn't recognize the voice. Dad kept saying that
he thought he had heard it before. He asked me several times,
"Dawn, don't you know that voice? I just can't quite place it,
but can't you?"

It was hopeless. The voice was too muffled. All we could
do was sit and wait.

5

FOR THE FIRST TIME SINCE SHARI'S DISAPPEARANCE, MOM, DAD, Robert, and I were persuaded by Captain Gasque of SLED to speak to the flock of reporters at the end of our driveway. Our emotions had been so raw that for the past three days we'd avoided the press. I didn't know what to expect from these people who so desperately wanted to be on top of "the story" that thousands of listeners waited for every night on the six o'clock news. But it wasn't a story to me and my family; it was our lives!

As we opened the front door and stepped out into the blazing June heat, each of us hoped that if the man who had Shari could see us on TV and know that we were desperately hurting, he would give her back to us.

When my father started to speak, I could see that the strain had begun to wear away the strong front he had maintained. As I stood there beside him, our arms around each other's sides, I thought I felt him trembling. I hated whoever was doing this to him, to us, and I breathed a prayer that God would give Dad strength and the right words to say.

"We just want to say to whoever has our daughter Shari, we want her back. We miss her. We love her. Please send her back home where she belongs." Hearing my father pleading

41

for Shari's safe return hurt me deeply. Mom and Dad looked shattered, as if the past four days had robbed them of everything. We still stood there together, holding on to each other as the flashes from the cameras doubled the blinding effect of the sun.

Because Shari and I looked so much alike, investigators decided to try and draw out the kidnapper by placing me out front during the press conference. Psychopaths often select victims that resemble each other. Their hunch would soon prove to be right.

Sheriff Metts then told reporters that the investigation was leading them to believe that Shari could still be alive and that somebody could be holding her. The members of the press buzzed with this new information as their pencils and pens scratched on note pads. Again, the rumors that Shari was already dead were corrected. We then climbed back into the patrol car and returned to the protection of our home.

Although we were there in the midst of it all, with the command post right in our front field, we still found ourselves wondering if the authorities were telling us everything. Every night at 6:00, Mom, Dad, Robert, and I would head to the den to watch the news to see if we'd missed anything. I began to hate the sound of the music for Channel 10. Its upbeat tune almost seemed to mock us.

Shari's senior picture was now plastered on every newspaper and news broadcast in sight. She looked so beautiful—her long blonde hair curled and hanging loosely, framing her perfect skin and blue eyes.

The news over, it was time to sit and wait once again. That seemed to be all we could do. A local sandwich shop brought croissants with ham and cheese, and Domino's delivered pizzas. A church friend, Gene Rountree, who owned a food services company, had food lockers and freezers placed in our double-car garage to feed all the officers, friends, and volunteers. We would eat, not really in meals, but just bites now and then when there was nothing else to do.

Then what we were waiting for came—a letter in the mail. It was definitely from Shari, in her own handwriting, but some of the things she said were very strange. In the left-hand corner appeared the date 6/1/85, and she'd drawn a little heart on the side of the page beside the words, "God is love." In the right-hand corner was 3:10 A.M. and "I love ya'll!" underlined three times. She had entitled the letter, "Last Will and Testament." She and her boyfriend, Richard, had made up this silly thing that they did with their names, combining them into one word, *ShaRichard*. That was on the other side of the first page. It was, without a doubt, from Shari.

> *I love you, Mommy, Daddy, Robert, Dawn, & Richard,*
> *and everyone else and all other friends and relatives. I'll*
> *be with my Father now, so please, please don't worry!*
> *Just remember my witty personality & great special*
> *times we all shared together. Please don't even let this*
> *ruin your lives, just keep living one day at a time for*
> *Jesus. Some good will come out of this. My thoughts*
> *will always be with you & in you! (casket closed)*

What did all this mean? This was definitely Shari's handwriting, but it didn't make sense. She went on to say:

> *I love you all so _____ much. Sorry, Dad, I had to*
> *cuss for once! Jesus forgave me!*

That was so like her. She was so strong-willed, and she knew Dad would not like her choice of words. Next came a personal note to Richard:

> *Richard sweetie—I really did & always will love you & treasure our special moments. I ask one thing though— accept Jesus as your personal Savior.*

There was a little smiley face after that sentence.

> *My family has been the greatest influence on my life. Sorry about the cruise money. Somebody please go in my place. I am sorry if I ever disappointed you in any way. I only wanted to make you proud of me because I have always been proud of my family. Mom, Dad, Robert, & Dawn, there's so much I want to say that I should have said before now. I love ya'll! I know ya'll love me and will miss me very much, but if ya'll stick together like we always did—ya'll can do it! Please do not become hard or upset. "Everything works out for the good for those that love the Lord." (Romans 8:28)*
>
> > *All my love always,*
> > *Sharon (Shari) F. Smith*
> > *I love ya'll w/all my heart!*
>
> *P.S. Nana—I love you so much. I kind of always felt like your favorite. You were mine! I love you a lot.*

As soon as we'd read it, the SLED agents sped the letter to the state crime laboratory for fingerprinting analysis, but the haunting words did not leave with them. I would not allow myself to see this letter as a last will and testament, and I could not stand the thought of my sister being in a casket now or ever. She seemed to be trying to tell us what was happening, but we could not face that possibility. The letter sounded as if she had so much to say and was trying to get it all on these two pages, but couldn't.

She may have been drugged at the time of the writing, but how could we know that? We went over and over the letter, clinging to it because it was something physical, something that she had touched with her own hands. We kept looking for clues, hidden clues, anything that she may have put in there to help us find her. But it seemed her main concern was us. She even told us not to worry about her. How could we not worry about her?

Inside I was crying. My prayers became more urgent as the hours passed. Then the ringing of the phone came again. I jumped instinctively at its first shrill sound.

"Hello," I said, out of breath from flying down the steep stairs into the kitchen.

"Dawn," came the voice I so dreaded to hear.

"Yes," I answered, trying to sound calm.

"Did you come down from Charlotte?" he asked, his voice still sounding as if he were using something to alter it.

"Yes, I did. Who's calling, please?" I asked, knowing all too well who it was, yet hoping he might give some clue.

"I need to speak to your mother," came the voice again, a bit nervous.

"Okay," I said, telling someone in the room to get Mom. "She's coming."

"Tell her to hurry."

"She's hurrying. Tell Shari I love her," I gasped, trying to get anything I could in to my sister and praying that she would get the message.

"Did ya'll receive her letter today?" he asked, seeming not as worried that Mom wasn't on the phone yet.

"Yes, we did. Here's Mother," I replied, hoping I was doing the right thing since he had seemed so intent on her getting there quickly before.

"Did you receive her letter today?"

"Yes, we did. Here's Mother," I said, trying not to sound agitated.

"Did you receive her letter today?" came the question for the third time.

Mother was now on the phone. "Pardon?" she said. "I can't hear you. It's not very clear. Speak louder."

"Did you receive the letter today?"

"Uh, yes, I did," my mother answered, her tone high and nervous.

"Tell me one thing it said," came the distorted voice.

My mother shakily began to tell him some of the things Shari had said. Groping to remember, she told him of the little heart drawn on the side, that the letter was two pages long on a yellow legal pad, and that it said "God is love" on the front page.

"Okay, so you know now this is not a hoax," came the flat, distorted voice.

"Yes, I know that," Mom said, trying to keep her composure.

He said something about "them" missing Sheriff Metts that morning after having instructed us to have the sheriff get on the news on Channel 10 and call off the search. Mom tried to make up an excuse.

"Okay," he went on, "I'm trying to do everything possible to answer some of your prayers, so please, in the name of God, work with us here—"

"All right," Mom interrupted. "Can you answer me one question, please. You—you are very kind and—and you seem to be a compassionate person and—and I think you know how I feel being Shari's mother and how much I love her. Can you tell me, is she all right physically without her medicine?"

"Shari is drinking a little over two gallons of water per hour and using the bathroom right afterwards," came the reply Mom wanted to hear.

"All right." Mom almost sighed in relief. "Is she able to eat? Because she usually doesn't eat. That—that's what concerns me."

"No," he said, as if he no longer cared to discuss Shari's condition. "Listen, I've got to hurry now."

"I know that." Mama tried to sound understanding.

"Okay, now, what I'm going to do is, uh, have an ambulance—now, this is very important. Have—this has gone too far. I'm—please forgive me. Uh, have an ambulance ready at anytime at your house . . . and on Shari's request, she requests that only immediate family come and Sheriff Metts and the ambulance attendants. She don't want to make a circus out of this." His voice now sounded even more high-pitched.

"Right," Mom said, just trying to go along with him to keep him on the phone.

Referring back to the letter, he added, "And where she said 'casket closed' in parenthesis . . . if anything happens to me, she said her—one of her requests she did not put in there, to put her hands on her stomach like she was praying in the casket."

"What now?" cried Mom, no longer able to hide her panic.

"Cross her hands . . ."

"Why would anything happen to you? We don't want any harm to you. I—I promise. We just want Shari well and all right, okay?" Mom's voice sounded tight and full of emotion.

"Okay. Now, does Sheriff Metts realize that this is not a hoax call?"

"Yes, he—he knows this is not a hoax," Mom said, once again trying to keep the unknown man calm and talking while struggling with her own fear.

"Okay. Well, tell him to just forget about all other suspects and the only thing—when I talked to you Monday morning 2:30 in the morning . . ."

"Yes."

". . . the first time?"

"Yes. I did not realize—I thought you were a police officer at first."

"Okay, listen. Listen real carefully. I've got to hurry. I know these calls are being traced, correct?" he asked, his voice sounding more agitated.

Mom told him that she didn't know. With her daughter's life depending on this phone call, she was willing to do anything to keep this person on the phone.

"They are," he seemed to answer for himself. "Okay, now listen, uh!" He seemed to be losing his train of thought.

Miraculously calm, Mom said, "I'm listening."

"Yeah, hold on a second."

"Are you still there?" Mom asked, thinking for a second that he might have hung up.

"Yes. Okay, hold on just a second."

"Uh." Mom tried to think of something to say to get him talking again. "Is Shari with you or can you tell me?"

"I will not say," came the cold reply.

"I—I can tell you're upset," Mom soothed him as he seemed to be losing control.

"Oh, yes, okay, hold on before I forget it. I told you that morning you were looking at the wrong place, right?"

"Yes, you did," Mom replied.

"I wish you would have remembered that, and I don't know why . . ." he said, his voice rising higher.

"I did remember that."

"Okay, well, listen to us, please. Okay, forget Lexington County. Look in Saluda County. Do you understand?"

"Look in Saluda County," Mom eagerly replied.

"Exactly. Uh, closest to Lexington County within a fifteen-mile radius right over the line. Is that understood?" he asked, still seeming irritated at the stupidity of the authorities for not following his instructions.

"Yeah."

"And please—very, very soon get—please, now Shari's request—Shari Faye requests please no strangers hardly and—when ya'll—when we give the location . . ." He seemed to be completely losing his train of thought.

Mom tried to go along with this senseless jumble of words. "No strangers absolutely."

"Okay, now did you understand about the folding of the hands like she was in prayer in case something happens to us?"

"Yes, if something happens to ya'll. But nothing—listen, nobody is going to harm you. I promise you that."

"Well, tell Sheriff Metts that he—I don't know what the

problem is. I told you to forget about looking around your house. Saluda County," he demanded.

"It—listen, there are . . ." Mom stuttered.

"Do you believe me now?" he asked, completely changing the subject.

"I believe you," Mom said in exasperation. "There are so many people—"

"I know that."

"—that love Shari and they just won't give up."

"Shari—I want to tell you one other thing," he said stiffly.

Mom, still trying to find some way of explaining why the search had continued in Lexington County said, "They just continue to look."

"I want to tell you one other thing. Shari is now a part of me. Physically, mentally, emotionally, spiritually. Our souls are one now."

In unbelief, Mom could only say, "Your soul is now one with Shari?"

"Yes, and we're trying to work this out, so please do what we ask. You haven't been doing that. I don't understand, and she doesn't. We sit here and watch TV and we see no sheriff. We—"

Mom interrupted, "Why doesn't Shari—Shari talk to me? She—knows me so well."

"That's why she asked me to communicate with you . . ."

"But—"

"Not your husband. Aren't you aware of that?" he asked.

"Yes, I know that. I—I know that she would ask you to talk with me."

"And—and she said she does love ya'll and like she said, 'Do not let this ruin your lives.'"

"We're not going to let it ruin our—"

"Okay, well . . ."

"But it—you tell—listen," Mom began. "You tell Shari one thing."

"What is it?" he asked, sounding interested.

"There's no way my life could ever be—have any happiness in it again if—if Shari left this world with me bearing a guilt that I—I had failed in such a bad way because I love her and I want to make her happy. I'll do anything . . ." Mom's voice broke with emotion.

"She knows that."

". . . to work it out. She doesn't have to come home. Okay?"

"Okay."

"I'm serious. She does not have to come home. Anything." Mom desperately wanted to make sure she covered every possibility, even though we all felt strongly that Shari was not there by her own choice.

"Well, time's up and, uh, please now have the ambulance ready at any time," came his instructions once again.

"At any time," was all Mom could say.

"This will not go any further and, uh, it will be soon." He sounded as if he truly cared about the heartbreak we were all going through.

"The ambulance . . ." Mom's voice suddenly filled with panic again. "You're not telling me that—"

"No."

"—something's going to happen to her, and I'm going to have an ambulance."

"I'm telling you her condition," he said, referring to the condition of her diabetes as far as Mom could understand.

"It's getting bad? Is that what you're—"

"You know more about it than I do."

"I know I do," she said frantically, "and that's why I am so worried about it."

"Well, you have the ambulance, and I'll give you the location, and tell Sheriff Metts to get all his men in Saluda County. Okay, well, God bless all of . . ."

"Will you call me soon?" Mom pleaded.

"I will," was his short reply.

"Will you call me back tonight? I—I just need reassurance to know that she's still okay."

"I have to be careful. I've got to go now and listen, uh, . . ."

"Will you?"

"Please, please, please, forgive me for this. It just got out of hand." He seemed agitated again.

"I know. Listen, do me one thing," Mom requested, hoping to calm the man.

"What's that? Hurry."

"Just tell Shari—I know she knows how much I love her. Tell her that her daddy loves her, and her daddy will work anything out with her under the sun and—and he admits we've got a lot of problems, and we'll work them out, and her brother and sister love her and . . ."

"Okay."

"God bless you for taking care of my baby," Mom sobbed.

"Shari is protected and like you said, she is part of me now and God looks after all of us . . . good night."

Once again, the call was traced, but no one was found at the phone booth, though this had been the longest of the three calls. I was so proud of my mother for the way she kept this unknown man on the phone all that time. But it was almost more than Mom could take.

Later as I sat in my room with Cindy and Julie, it was dark outside and dark inside my heart. I kept asking them, God, and myself why all this was happening. Was I to blame in any way? I knew my relationship with God had not been right this past year. I began to plead with Him, telling Him I'd do anything if only He'd let Shari live.

I had been a "good kid" all the way through school. When I was in the eighth grade, we had moved from Columbia, SC, to Lexington because Dad wanted to raise his family in the country, as he'd been raised. The new kid on the block, I was not accepted. I did not get into the drugs, alcohol, and promiscuity so common in the school—partly because my parents had raised us so strictly and partly because of my own commitment to the Lord. The other kids would call me names and even threatened to burn our house down one night when my family was asleep. Practically every day that year, I came home in tears and rushed into the bathroom before my mother could see me.

As I went on to high school, it became a little easier, but not much. I was by no means popular, but my friends at school were from my church youth group. We stood together against the crowd. Things that seemed to be such a temptation to my classmates didn't even entice me. I wanted to do what was right.

But when I went to work at Carowinds, I gradually began to go along with my co-workers. I found myself being less vocal about my commitment to Jesus, and I even joined in with the drinking with the gang now and then. The atmosphere there was so different from what I'd been used to. I hated what I was doing, and the guilt would not go away. However, the group still called me "Little Miss Innocent." And I was, compared to them. Yet while I wasn't doing anything terrible, in my heart I knew I was displeasing God. And Shari knew it, for she had seen what I was doing.

Shari had always been the mischievous one, and I was more conservative. To her I was boring. Her favorite way of describing me was to call me a "goody-goody," but I didn't really care. It was pretty much the truth. I was always more concerned about doing what was right, and she was interested in doing whatever it was she wanted to do at the moment— and pay later. We were opposites, but still we had a very special relationship.

Now I couldn't bear the thought of having let her down. I would constantly beg God to let her live so that I could tell her how sorry I was and make it up to her—be the sister she could be proud of. Julie, Cindy, and I would pray over and over together for Shari's safety. And I would pray, *Oh, God, please give me that chance, just one more chance.*

6

MORNING, TUESDAY, JUNE 4, CAME, AND WITH IT THE NEWSPA-
pers. There we were—Mom, Dad, Robert, and I—on the front
page of *The State*. Beside us was Shari's picture. She looked so
beautiful, and we looked so frazzled and broken. Robert had
on his Carolina baseball hat, and I had on a short-sleeved
sweatshirt with hearts all over it. Those hearts reminded me
of the heart Shari had drawn on the side of her letter. Dad
looked grief-stricken, and Mom's face couldn't really be seen
in the shadow of Robert's tall body as he stood beside her, his
arm around her, but her body was slouched as if she were an
old woman.

The headline read, "SHERIFF THINKS TEEN IS STILL ALIVE.
MISSING GIRL'S FAMILY PLEADS FOR HER SAFE RETURN." We
stood where Shari's car had been left as she went to get the
mail. Our two-story brick house with its two wooden dorm-
ers looked almost like a doll house in the distance. The story
went on to tell about the two ambulances that had arrived at
our house around 8:45 the night before at the kidnapper's
orders. These had been parked behind our house all night as
we had waited for the man to call back with "the location."
The press was not to be told why they were there.

The article described a Columbia man, age twenty-seven,

who was arrested Saturday morning for calling our home and demanding a ransom. That man cost the sheriff's department a lot of man-hours and us a lot of unnecessary pain. I was glad he had been apprehended.

A nationwide alert to all law enforcement agencies had brought a few inquiries from other states where women had recently been abducted under similar circumstances. They were all being checked out.

"Throughout the three-day search," wrote Peter O'Boyle III of *The State*, "passing motorists have stopped at the Smiths' home to inquire about the case or to ask authorities if they need any help."

And indeed they had. On Monday the driver of an eighteen-wheeler tractor-trailer stopped and asked a deputy directing traffic in front of the house, "Did you find her?" The deputy silently shook his head no.

The 100 to 150 law enforcement officers were continuing the search and had once again requested volunteers. By this time, they had covered a minimum area of twenty-five miles around our home. More than 10,000 posters with Shari's picture had been printed by a private group, and volunteers were distributing them today in hopes that someone who might have missed the news broadcasts could possibly know something.

It promised to be another long, hot day of restless waiting. Friends continued to come, but had to be cleared at the checkpoint at the entrance to our twenty-acre property. Early on, I heard the name Mark Heckle come over the walkie-talkie. He was a family friend and my date for my first prom. I was so glad to hear he was coming. I knew he would lift our spirits.

I watched him walk down our long driveway and saw that

he was not alone. I recognized the man with him, but could not recall his name. They came in, and Mark and I hugged. "I thought you could probably use a pizza about now," he announced cheerfully.

It was not just a pizza, but it was a *Pizza Hut* pizza, pepperoni. On practically all of our dates during high school, Mark and I had frequented one place, Pizza Hut.

He introduced his friend as Will Jordan. I remembered seeing Will at church a few times. He, I guessed, was somewhere around my age—with brown hair, muscular build, handsome face, and kind blue-green eyes—a very good-looking guy. He played drums in a Christian rock band with some of the other guys in our church.

As we sat in the den sharing pizza, Mark, Will, Robert, and I talked and laughed. The guys took turns putting the golf ball into the inside portable golf hole. For a few short moments, we were able to escape from the horror of our situation. I saw my brother smile for the first time in days. Those moments were very special.

After Mark and Will left, it was back to the normal schedule of waiting. Waiting. Waiting. As the afternoon sun began to disappear behind the trees, we listened to the Channel 10 news. But there was no news. I got up to go to my room. I dreaded passing Shari's room on the way to mine. Hers was a disaster, and I had to fight to keep from being infuriated with the people who had done the damage. Every single drawer, every corner of her closet, under her twin beds—everything had been gone through. Even her Bible had been searched for clues. Her notebooks from school and all her letters, even love letters to and from Richard, had been read. I hated this invasion of my sister's privacy. Fingerprint dusting powder covered the tops of her furniture, as well as her mirror—with its photos of her and Richard at the prom and of our cat, Tabby, stuck in the frame.

Exhaustion overcame me. I desperately needed to sleep, but a solid night's sleep was impossible. Sounds from downstairs and the overall worry would not permit it. I pleaded with God to hurry up and end this terrible ordeal.

I was afraid to take a shower lest the phone should ring. I didn't even go the bathroom unless I absolutely couldn't wait any longer. And no sooner had I made my way upstairs than it did ring. Down I flew. Breathless, I grabbed the receiver and gasped, "Hello."

"Uh, Dawn?" came the dreaded voice.

"Yes."

"Uh, this is Shari Faye's request. Get your mother on the phone quickly." I was so tired of him telling me to do things quickly when he was the one dragging this whole thing out.

"Get on the other phone, Mother," I ordered nervously. She was just inches away from me, as was everyone by the time I had picked up the phone.

"Get a pencil and piece of paper ready," he commanded.

"Get a pencil and paper ready," I quickly told one of the deputies standing nearby.

"She's not on the phone yet," I said, referring to Mom.

"Well, I'll tell *you* this."

"Okay," was all I knew to say. I wasn't sure that I was ready for one more word from this man.

"Uh, are you aware that was in Shari's own handwriting?" he said, referring to her letter.

"Yes, I am. All right."

"Okay, now this is Shari's own words." Was I actually going to hear from Shari—her own voice?

"Okay." I anxiously waited.

"So listen carefully. Say nothing unless you're asked."

"Okay," I said, intent on hearing anything from my sister.

"Okay, and it's not necessary—I know these calls are taped . . ."

"Uh-huh." Not knowing what to say, I fumbled.

He continued, ". . . and traced, but that's irrelevant now. There's no money demanded, so here's Shari Faye's last request. On the fifth day to put the family at rest, Shari Faye being freed. Remember, we are one soul now. When you locate—when located, you'll locate us both together. We are one. God has chosen us. Respect all past and present requests. Actual events and times—jot this down. Hurry."

"All right, I'm doing it." I was writing and listening as fast as I could. Although the calls were being recorded, I was writing just in case something went wrong with the machine. I couldn't take a chance on missing anything.

"3:28 in the afternoon," came a fragmented sentence. "Friday, 31st of May, Shari—"

"Wait a minute," I interrupted. "Too fast. 3:28 afternoon . . ."

". . . Shari Faye was kidnapped from your mailbox with a gun. She had the fear of God in her, and she was at the mailbox. That's why she did not return back to her car."

"She had—she had to fear what?" I wasn't quite sure I had gotten it all.

"Fear of God."

"Fear of God," I repeated.

"Okay," he continued, as if he were reading a manuscript.

"4:48 A.M.—no, I'm sorry. Hold on a minute. 3:10 A.M., Saturday, the first of June, uh, she hand-wrote what you received. 4:58 A.M., Saturday, the first of June . . ."

"Okay, Saturday, the first of June, 4:58 A.M." I was trying so desperately to understand all his mumbling.

As if he didn't even hear me, he continued, ". . . became one soul."

"Became one soul," I again repeated.

"What does that mean?" my mother's panic-filled voice interrupted from her phone.

"No questions now." He seemed aggravated with her for interrupting.

"All right," she agreed.

"Last, between 4:00 and 7:00 Wednesday, tomorrow, have ambulance ready. Remember, no circus." He gave the same orders as before.

"4:00 and . . ." was all I could get out.

"Prayer . . ."

"Wait," I commanded. I could not get it all. "4:00 and 7:00 A.M.?"

"4:00 and 7:00 in the afternoon tomorrow," he answered as if I were an idiot.

"In the afternoon."

"Tomorrow."

"Okay," I said, relieved that at least I had gotten that much.

"Okay," he continued, "have an ambulance ready. Remember her request. No circus."

Our front yard had looked like a circus for the past five days with the big tent. I couldn't help thinking that this whole thing was in some ways a circus, as everyone watched our lives being totally destroyed.

"Okay," was all I could say.

"Prayers and relief coming soon. Please learn to enjoy life. Forgive. God protects the chosen. Shari Faye's important request: Rest tonight and tomorrow. Good shall come out of this. And please tell Sheriff Metts, search no more. Blessings are near. Remember, tomorrow, Wednesday, 4:00—4:00 in the afternoon until 7:00 in the evening. Ambulance ready. No circus."

"Okay, no circus. What does this mean?" I had to know. His crazy language was more than I could stand.

"You will receive last instructions where to find us. Please—"

"Okay, don't . . ." I interrupted, afraid he was going to hang up without my getting a grasp on what was going to happen.

". . . forgive . . ."

"Do not kill my daughter, PLEASE!" Mom begged, no longer able to constrain her terror.

"We love and miss ya'll. Get . . ."

"Let me—" Mom began, but he wouldn't let her finish.

". . . good rest tonight."

"Listen—" Mom's voice rose.

"Good-bye."

"Wait a minute!" Mom practically screamed.

"He's gone, Mama," I said quietly. He had already hung up.

The call had come in at 9:49 P.M. It was the most terrifying one of all. Authorities feared it was an ominous hint of a murder-suicide. They traced it to a phone booth over at Jake's Landing at Lake Murray, but again they could not get there in time. Officers from at least four law enforcement agencies set up roadblocks immediately on both sides of the Lake Murray dam. An air and ground pursuit followed, with patrol cars and a helicopter searching several vehicles sighted near the Fast Fare convenience store. Fingerprints were taken from the phone booth, and authorities at the scene showed a composite drawing of a suspect to witnesses. But by 11:30 searchers admitted that the caller had eluded them. Why couldn't they catch him when the calls had been traced every time, I wondered. My patience was wearing thin.

Now we could no longer hold back the terror hidden in our hearts. Mom's plea, "Do not kill my daughter. PLEASE!" played over and over in my head like a broken record, as did Shari's haunting words, "casket closed," along with the caller's hated voice. What had he meant about Shari and he being "one soul now" and "we are one" and "God has chosen us"? It was like something out of a horror movie where you can't make sense out of any of it until the very end. But I didn't want to think about the ending.

No longer could I remember anything good that had ever happened in my life. All that had been before this moment, frozen in time, was gone. I was ready to break out of the prison that our house had become and find Shari myself.

7

ANOTHER SLEEPLESS NIGHT OF TOSSING AND TURNING WAS COM-ing to an end. As I lay awake in my big, white iron bed, listening to the sounds of the law officers who had worked around the clock downstairs, I decided to get up. Maybe if I got out of bed, took a shower, and ate some breakfast, I'd feel better. Once downstairs, the feeling I was hoping for didn't come. The all-too-familiar faces of the officers who had lived with us for the past five days, going on six, summoned again the feelings of despair, fear, helplessness, and exhaustion. Suddenly the thought of breakfast made me feel nauseated.

June 5, 1985. Was it going to pass like all the other days? That morning authorities were working on laying an elaborate trap to shut down pay telephones throughout much of Columbia, forcing the kidnapper to hunt for working phones in areas under concentrated surveillance.

Please, God, I prayed silently, *please let us find out something about Shari today. My parents can't take much more of this.* The hardest part was not knowing how Shari was. It had been too many days since her last medication. Without it, she couldn't eat anything due to nausea. We knew she would suffer from the lack of proper treatment even if she were getting enough water. The hormone deficiency in her type of diabetes caused her kidneys to race out of control, and any water she drank would drain immediately. We could only pray that the kidnapper was taking care of her as he'd said in one of the phone calls. I couldn't remember which one, since they were all running together in my mind. Would he call today? I hoped so. I dreaded hearing that awful voice, but I needed some assurance about my sister.

I hovered near the phone constantly, waiting for its shrill clamor. At 11:54 it came. I caught it after only one ring.

"Hello."

"Listen carefully," he began. I knew it was going to be him. No other calls were to come through on that line, and by now, most of our friends, relatives, and other concerned people knew not to call.

He continued, "Take Highway 378 west to the traffic circle. Take Prosperity exit, go one and a half miles, turn right at sign, Moose Lodge #103, go one-quarter mile, turn left at white framed building, go to back yard. Six feet beyond we're waiting. God chose us."

Click. He hung up without even giving me a chance to respond to his directions. He'd called only fifteen minutes before the phones were to be cut off! I lifted my eyes to Captain Gasque, certain that the fear of what those directions would lead to would be in his eyes, too. He looked over the notes I'd scribbled down as best I could while the sheriff rewound the tape. As we listened, it was evident that the man had been reading from a note that he must have made for himself. His voice held no emotion.

Captain Gasque then fixed us with a look of deep compassion. "Would you come upstairs with me?"

We filed up to my bedroom where Mom, Dad, and Robert

sat down on the bed, and I took the straight chair by the door. Captain Gasque stood in the doorway. "I think it would be best," he suggested, "if you would wait up here out of the way of the rest of the household while we check this out."

Mom quickly jumped up. "I need to pack a bag for her to take to the hospital."

"Uh, Mrs. Smith," Captain Gasque said gently, "don't worry about that now. We can get it later."

But Mom refused to listen. She stuffed Shari's favorite nightgown, toothbrush, and medicine in a bag. Mom didn't want her beautiful daughter, who'd been through only God knew what, to have to wear those uncomfortable and drafty hospital gowns. As she gave the bag to Captain Gasque, a flicker of hope ran through me. They would rescue Shari and bring her back to us. But then the same fear that I'd lived with for the past five days took over. We sat in silence, as the sound of my heartbeat pounded in my ears like the slow ticking of the seconds going by.

The silence was unbearable, yet there was nothing to say. I think all four of us were praying harder than ever that Shari would be found and that she would be alive. I remembered the verse in the Bible that proclaimed that with God nothing is impossible. Yet in addition to her life-threatening disease, I knew that her kidnapper might have abused her.

This waiting was unlike all the rest. At least I felt that we'd find out something when it came to an end. But what? Hadn't I prayed that today we'd find out *something* concerning the whereabouts of my sister . . . anything? Now I wished I hadn't made that request. *I didn't really mean "anything," God,* I prayed.

After some time, I heard the sound of a car pulling up in

the driveway. My heart began to beat too rapidly to sit comfortably, but I didn't dare stand up lest I make my family more afraid. The footsteps climbing those familiar stairs seemed to be in slow motion. Captain Gasque appeared in the doorway, and the look on his face told us everything.

All of a sudden my mother cried out, "My baby, oh, God, my baby!"

"We found her body behind the Masonic Lodge," the captain said gently.

"Are you sure it's Shari?" Dad choked out.

"There could be no mistake."

The captain said something about how sorry he was and then turned to leave us alone. I did not move from my chair. My mother continued that horrible wailing as Dad tried to hold her, and Robert just sat there and began to whimper. I didn't want to believe it. I wanted to see her for myself. Captain Gasque had said also that it would not be necessary for any of the family members to identify the body. He said that it was in too bad a condition, and he would not allow us to go. They were certain it was my sister.

Tears wouldn't come. I just sat there dazed, in shock, as if I'd never be able to feel again. Mom and Dad were crying with the most beastlike, mournful sounds I'd ever heard. I wanted to go over to them and to hug my brother who sat alone, crying, but I couldn't. Finally tears began to fill my own eyes, and my family faded into an ugly blur before me. Was Shari really dead? My beautiful sister, her life now over . . . one that had held such promise? Her future completely wiped out by some crazed madman? At that moment, I wished it had been my life that had ended, so that I would not have to go on any further in this tragic nightmare.

I don't remember how long we were in that room. It seemed as if I had been sitting in that chair all my life. I couldn't stand the thought of my beautiful, happy-go-lucky sister being left outside in the tremendous heat like some heap of garbage. She was a human being full of love, feelings, talents, emotions, and dreams. Now all of that was over.

Who had done this to her? I wanted him found, and I didn't want to wait one more day. Would he call again? If so, how could I handle talking to the man who had done this to my sister and my family? Yet if he didn't call, would he ever be caught? *Oh, Lord, they have to catch him,* I commanded God. But I was tired of asking for things.

As I made my way down the steep stairs, dizziness overcame me. Had I stood up too quickly, or was it shock? Julie met me at the bottom with open arms, an agonizing expression on her face. She just held me as we cried together. There were no words that could possibly ease the unbearable pain. She had loved Shari as much as she loved her own sisters.

As I opened my eyes and looked over Julie's shoulder, now soaked with my tears, I saw Cindy just standing there, helplessly. No one knew what to do. How could life ever hold any joy or promise again, I wondered. My singing career didn't matter anymore. Nothing mattered except Shari. All I'd thought about and prayed about was Shari and her safe return. Now that hope was gone. I had nothing.

God, how could You? Why would You let this happen to us? How could You let Shari suffer? Oh, God, how much she must have suffered! Did You even listen to my constant prayers all this time? Didn't You hear anything I said? Evidently not! You could have stopped this from happening, couldn't You? Of course He could

67

have stopped it, but He didn't. *Thanks a lot, God, for nothing,* I shouted in my mind!

Up the stairs I flew into that bedroom that I never wanted to enter again, but there was nowhere else to go. I flung myself on my bed where my mother and father had groaned and wailed. The room that had once been a place of peace and solace was no longer that for me. I hated it. All the pretty pastel flowers on the matching curtains and bedspreads that Nana and Papa Smith had given me (like the ones in Shari's room in blues and beige), the pink wall that I'd painted myself so proudly, and all the dolls I'd collected over the years seemed to be mocking me. This was no longer the beautiful room I'd been so proud to show my friends. It was the dreadful place where I had learned of the end of a beautiful, priceless life that could never be brought back.

I WAS AWAKENED BY THE FAMILIAR SOUNDS OF POLICE RADIOS, walkie-talkies, and officers talking in hushed tones. I distinctly heard FBI Agent John Douglas saying that "he" was jerking everybody around like puppets, that there was no doubt we were dealing with a psycho, and that I was their best bet for snaring him. As they continued to discuss the case, I no longer felt any urgency. It all was hopeless now. Even if they caught the monster who did this horrible thing, it wouldn't bring my sister back. The hopes, small as they were, that Shari would come through the front door again with her brilliant, dimpled smile were dead.

The letter! Had she actually known she was going to die when she wrote it to us? I had refused to believe it even though her words were so final. Shari was a fighter, and she wouldn't give up until the very end. Had she already known what her fate would be? I tried to remember each word. How I wanted to mark them in my memory forever. She must have told us that she loved us five times. Could she actually have known it would be the last time she'd ever say those words? There had been no trace of fear in her letter, and maybe that's why I believed she was just writing it because she was told to.

There were no more tears left in me to cry. My heart was

frozen, seemingly never to feel again. My chest ached from heaving. My throat felt as if it would swell completely shut from choked emotion. Maybe it would just close up so that I couldn't breathe anymore, and all this pain would be over!

Where had Mom, Dad, and Robert gone? I cared, but I had nothing to offer them. I felt I couldn't help or be helped. My mother's words to the kidnapper rang over and over in my ears. "There's no way my life could ever be—have any happiness in it again if . . ." That was exactly how I felt. The world as I'd known it was gone. Roses would always look dead to me. The grass would always be withered, and even on the brightest summer days, a cloud would cover the earth. I would never laugh again with my sister, who had such a great sense of humor. She had the rare ability to bring light into the middle of the darkest day. Now who would there be to do that?

My thoughts finally shut off sometime in the late afternoon, and I slept fitfully, passing back and forth from dreams to reality. Did I hear the phone ring? No, it must have been my imagination. I knew I must do something, but I couldn't think past the walls of my bedroom. Slowly, feeling weighted down as if I were under water, I raised myself up from my bed. My body felt so tired. I knew I needed to eat something, but the thought of food made me nauseous.

As I made my way down the stairs, I felt as if all eyes were on me. All those friends and family members who had done so much for us now seemed a nuisance. What were they all still doing there? Didn't they have their own lives to get back to now that ours were over?

In the kitchen, Julie tried to fix me a sandwich and something to drink. I tried to eat, but the bites were hard to swallow. Hopelessness enveloped me. Shari's words about living one day at a time for Jesus came to mind again. Living for Jesus? Hadn't I prayed in His name just like the Bible told me to do? Then why hadn't He answered my prayers? I'd begged on my hands and knees for Him to let Shari live. Now I felt humiliated. I had actually believed that He would save her. Where had He been during this entire nightmare? I had no prayers left in me. I had been so consumed with praying for Shari's life that now that it was over, I had nothing left to say to God. To tell the truth, I didn't know if He was even there at all anymore, and I didn't want to waste my breath if He wasn't. I felt empty.

●

I awoke the next morning with my stomach growling and the smell of coffee coming from downstairs. What would this day hold? Nothing, I presumed. Just another day to exist in a meaningless world.

On the way down the hall, I stopped by the door to Robert's bedroom to find him still sleeping. I was glad. I hoped he'd sleep well into the day if he could. At least then he was out of his misery.

The house was quiet. I made my way over to the counter to get some cereal. I asked someone where Mom was, and they told me that she was still sleeping. I guessed the sedatives had helped. Dad was up, and I could tell by the way his face looked, so drawn with worry and grief, that he'd slept little. I went over and hugged him weakly. I feared that every time he'd look at me from now on, it would be a reminder of the other daughter he'd had. People had always said Shari and I looked alike, and sometimes when we were younger, they even asked if we were twins. Often Mom would dress us alike. We always said we hated it although we really didn't. Today I would have given anything to once again put on the matching dresses we wore when we sang together . . . I pushed the thoughts aside.

The State newspaper lay on the kitchen table. "POLICE HUNT 'SICK' KILLER," headlines declared on the front page. "BODY OF MISSING TEENAGER FOUND IN SALUDA COUNTY," continued the article. There was a picture of the lodge where my precious sister's body had been found, left out in the back like some animal run over by a car.

"Investigators in three counties were searching for a 'very sick individual' who led authorities to believe Shari Smith was still alive before telephoning the teenager's family with the specific location of her body," the first paragraph began. "A preliminary autopsy indicated Miss Smith probably had been dead since Saturday—the day before she was to have graduated from Lexington High School." Oh, God, I couldn't bear to go on! But from somewhere deep inside me I suddenly felt a new surge of energy welling up. I wanted whoever was responsible to be caught immediately, and I wanted him to pay for what he'd done. In that instant I felt more anger, hate, and rage than in all the rest of my life put together.

The article went on to tell about how an unknown man had called our home and told us where Shari could be found. Authorities in a helicopter spotted her body around 12:35 P.M., just sixteen miles from our home. Just sixteen miles! She'd been so close. Why hadn't the authorities been able to find her before now? The article continued with a quote from Sheriff Metts saying that he believed Shari had been murdered with "some kind of instrument," but the autopsy report stated that no signs of injury to the body had been found. Dr. Joel Sexton, the Newberry forensic pathologist, also said that it did not appear that she had been shot, stabbed, or beaten. At least I could breathe a sigh of relief there.

Because Shari's body was in an "advanced state of decomposition," no cause of death could be determined, but she was definitely murdered. Metts said that if she did, in fact, die on Saturday, our family doctor did not believe her diabetic condition was the cause.

The coroner said that there were no signs that Shari had been injured or sexually assaulted. How I hoped that were true. She had been found barefoot, wearing her yellow swimsuit, white pullover shirt, and white shorts. Somehow, just knowing she was dressed when they found her brought me some comfort. The shirt had been pulled over her body "like a shroud," and she was lying face up about fifty feet from the back of the lodge.

Metts said the kidnapper "is a very sick individual who's playing games, no question, getting a lot of enjoyment out of jerking us around, and not only the police, but the family as well."

There was no question in my mind that he was enjoying torturing us. *Oh, God! Please help the police catch this maniac,* I screamed inside. *Okay, God, I know You're there, but I don't understand all this.* I had been used to praying in all circumstances of life, and I still felt compelled to, as angry as I was at God. Even if I didn't want to admit He was still in control, I knew He was and that He was listening to my every word. He had come into my heart at age nine, and He had promised

He'd never leave. From somewhere deep within I knew that He was the only One who could help me now.

●

I sat in disbelief. I couldn't fathom the task that had to be accomplished. Shari's funeral arrangements had to be made. I would never have guessed I would have to help plan my younger sister's funeral. I was thinking, *I will never be in my sister's wedding, crying joyfully as she walks down the aisle in her flowing gown. Instead, I'll cry tears of anguish at her funeral.*

The ride to the Caughman-Harman Funeral home was somber. I don't really remember anything specific about our time in that big, white house other than how badly I wanted to hurry up and get out of there. A family in our church had also tragically lost a child, their youngest son, a few years earlier. Mickey and Susan Wingard had showed such strong faith during that time. Now they had offered to meet us at the funeral home to help us with the details. The sweet spirit and obvious love for the Lord they showed made the painful time in that place more bearable.

We chose a lovely silver casket and pink roses to cover the top. The color pink reminded me of Shari. Thousands of people in the town of Lexington had tied pink ribbons on their mailboxes in memory of her. It was called the "Pink Ribbon Crusade." It stood for "People Really Care." Many cars displayed pink bumper stickers.

Of course Shari's request for a closed casket would be honored, not just because she wanted it that way, but because we had no other choice. The dress Mom had chosen for her to be buried in, her blue one that she'd worn for Homecoming, couldn't even be put on her, but had to be laid across her piti-fully decomposed body.

I continually had to push out of my mind the thoughts of how horrible her body must have looked when they found her. I was grateful that I'd only remember her as she was—beautiful, vivacious, full of life, happy, laughing, singing . . . was she singing right now? Was she singing more beautifully than she ever had before? I hoped so. She was with the Lord, singing to Him. The comfort of that thought brought peace to my troubled heart. Shari was with Jesus now, just as she'd written. As much as I hated her being gone from us, God let me know in my heart of hearts that she was in a better place. Although I didn't understand why it had to happen the tragic way it did, I knew that she'd never suffer again.

I wondered if exhaustion would ever leave me as I made my way back into the house that had become our prison. With nothing to do but wait, I found myself just wandering aim-lessly around the house. Julie had to go back to her baby-sit-ting job. Cindy had to return to Charlotte to her job at Carowinds. Loneliness settled into my spirit. It seemed every-one else's life was getting back to normal. Would mine ever?

I remembered Shari's letter. "Just keep living one day at a time for Jesus." She had never really been one to talk in that manner. I only guessed that when she was facing death, all things came into proper focus. The only things that matter are the things we do for Jesus. She knew she'd given her heart to Jesus as a little girl and that He would take care of her. She wasn't worried about herself—only about us. "Ya'll can do it . . . ya'll can do it . . . can do it . . . can do . . . can." How did Shari have such assurance?

I made my way up the familiar steps, past her bedroom,

and into mine. I picked up the Book that had been so precious to me since I'd asked Jesus to come into my heart. I was searching, looking for a way to make it. It was as if God directed my hands to Philippians. Desperate for an answer, I couldn't believe what I was reading. It said, "I can do all things through Christ who strengthens me" (4:13). I knew this verse was just for me. I didn't know how, or how long it might take, but if Shari somehow knew we could make it, I had to believe that I could. With a heart still broken and full of questions, I claimed that verse. "All things" had to mean all things. The catch had to be "through Christ who strengthens me." I knew my strength was long gone, but that God never becomes weary or tired. I would get through this with His strength, not my own. A new surge of hope ran through me, and somehow I knew I was going to make it!

9

THE COOL NIGHT BREEZE FELT REFRESHING ON MY FACE. I JUST
had to get outside for a minute. Besides, Lady needed to be let
out. Her constant barking at the confusion reminded us that
she did not like being locked up in the basement. She was such
a beautiful Great Dane, and I wrapped my arms around her
and hugged her. It was almost dark, but I knew I'd be okay if
I stayed right by the house, even though Mama and I had been
instructed by the police not to go outside without an officer. A
chill ran up my spine as I looked down to the woods behind
our house, past the pasture and the barn. The thought that
someone could be down there watching us brought back that
feeling of terror.

"Dawn! Dawn!" I jumped at the sound of Dad screaming
my name. He sounded mad. "Where are you?"

"Here I am." I fumbled my way back into the basement
and up the stairs into the kitchen.

"What were you doing? Where were you? Don't you know
better than to go outside of the house without telling anyone?"
he practically shouted. "Get the phone!"

"Here's Dawn right now," my Aunt Beverly was saying
with fear in her voice. I knew who it was.

"Hello," I said, out of breath.

"Dawn?"

"Yes."

"I'm calling for Shari Faye, and are you aware I'm turning myself in tomorrow morning?" came the voice I was trying not to hate with all that was in me.

"No," was all I could get out.

Sheriff Metts was next to me, monitoring the call with his headset.

"Well, have you talked to Sheriff Metts or Charlie Keyes?" he asked. Who was Charlie Keyes? Wasn't he some newscaster? What did he have to do with anything?

Confused, I replied, "Uh, no."

"Well, talk to them and listen carefully."

I was so sick of him giving me orders. I wanted to scream at him for what he'd done to Shari. "Okay," I agitatedly said.

"I have to tell you this, that uh, Shari asked me to, uh, turn myself in on the—the fifth day after they found her." His voice now sounded as if it were his own—unaltered—a sign of his growing confidence. He sickened me.

"Wait. Okay, I'm trying to write this down." I frantically took notes in case the recorder didn't work.

"Don't write it down," he commanded.

"Don't write it down?"

"Don't write it down," he repeated.

"Okay." I continued to hold the pen in my hand, ready to take notes.

"And, uh, or get myself straight with God and, uh, turn myself completely over to Him, so I have to turn myself over to Him." He seemed to be picking up right where he'd left off from notes of his own.

"Okay." *Just keep talking,* I thought.

"And, uh, they'll—uh, Charlie Keyes—you'll know what I'm talking about when you talk to him. We will not be able to get a personal interview from me in the morning. I'm, uh, they'll be a letter. It's already been mailed. An exact copy for you and for him and it's—with pictures." He paused.

"A copy to me?"

"Yes," he continued, "and him at his home of pictures of Shari Faye from the time—even—I made her stand up to her car and took two pictures and all through the thing, and the letter will describe exactly what happened from the time I picked her up until the time, uh, I called and told ya'll where to find her."

"Okay." I was still writing fiercely.

"And I'll be doing the same in the morning at 6:00, and tell the Sheriff and Charlie Keyes—Charlie Keyes, I used him as a medium today and I talked to him."

Going back over my notes, I repeated, "Okay, 6:00 A.M. What will you be doing in the morning?"

"Well, he'll know," came his short answer.

"Oh, he'll—"

"He'll already know," he broke in.

I wanted to scream. What was he talking about?

"Okay, and also that, uh, uh, that I will be armed, but by the time they find me, I won't be dangerous," he said.

"You—you . . ." I didn't know what to say. Was he going kill himself?

"Do you understand that?"

I read it back to him, "You will be armed—"

He interrupted, "But by the time they find me, I won't be dangerous."

"What does that mean?" I was tiring quickly of his little game.

"Well, I—Shari Faye said if I couldn't live with myself, and she wouldn't forgive me if I didn't turn myself over and turn myself in or turn myself over to God. So I'm going to have to— I just—this thing got out of hand and all I wanted to do was make love to Dawn. I've been watching her for a couple of—"

"To whom?" I panicked.

"To," he continued, "I'm sorry, to Shari. And I watched her a couple of weeks and, uh, it just got out of hand and, Dawn— Dawn, I hope you and your family forgive me for this."

How dare he ask such a thing, I thought. "You're not going to kill yourself, are you?"

"I—I don't—I can't live in prison and go to the electric chair. I can't do that. I—this is the only way I can get myself straight. I'm very sick and—but I—I can't go through . . ." he mumbled.

I felt no pity in my heart. I didn't think I could stand his whimpering to me about what he might have to go through after what he'd done to my sister. Regaining my control, I remembered I was to keep him on the line so they could trace the call. I said, "We don't want you to die. We want to help you. Don't kill yourself," with no sincerity in my voice.

"No," he muttered. "Oh, just, uh, you can't take someone's life, and this is the way it's going to have to be. Shari said—"

"Well, see, listen to me, okay?" I interrupted.

"Well, listen, I have to go."

"No," I demanded. I knew that if he hung up, we might never hear from him or find him. "I've got to tell you something, okay? This is important."

"Well, I know these calls . . ."

80

He was trying to change the subject, and I was starting to fear that I might lose him. "God can—"

". . . are being traced," he continued his sentence.

"God—well, that's okay. But God can forgive you and erase all of that." I couldn't believe what I was saying. But I knew it was the truth, and I hoped it would keep him from ending his life so we could find him.

"Dawn." He sounded as if he were beginning to cry. "I can't—I can't live with myself . . ."

"And we can forgive you, too," I said. Maybe if he knew we'd forgive him, he would listen.

". . . in prison for the rest of my life or go to the electric chair." It seemed he didn't even hear what I was saying.

He needed to be calmed down, so I said, "Listen, Shari's at peace with God. She's better off than any of us."

"Well, I want to say something to you that she told me."

Oh, I couldn't wait to hear even one mere word that came from her mouth. "Okay."

"Shari—oh boy." He seemed to be choking on his words. "Shari Faye said that, uh—she did not cry the entire time. She was very strong-willed, and she said that, uh, she did not want ya'll to ruin your lives and go on with your lives like the letter said. And I've never lied to ya'll before, right?"

"Yes," I said doubtfully.

"Okay," he continued, "so this is going to have to be the way it is, and she said that, uh, she wasn't scared—that she knew that she was going to be an angel and if I took the latter choice that she suggested to me, that she would forgive me, but our God's going to be the major judgment, and she'll probably end up seeing me in Heaven, not in Hell. And that, uh, she requests—now please remember this. Now, she requests that ya'll be sure to take her hands and fold them in her—on her stomach like she's praying . . ."

"Okay." I wanted him to go on.

"Okay. And please have Charlie Keyes with Sheriff Metts, and Charlie knows what to do in the morning and have an ambulance and probably—before they get there, they might as well have a hearse also and, uh, be at the traffic circle."

"The . . ."

"And I'm not in—I'll be—I'm just going to allow myself enough time to get in the area and get set up. I'm not in the area now. And, uh, it'll be 6:00 in the morning that I'll call his office and by the time they reach me, I'll be straight with God and, uh, Shari said please take the gold necklace that she had on and the—she had one earring in her left ear . . ."

Go on, go on, I wanted to say. I wanted to know everything Shari had possibly said to him. "Uh-uh."

". . . and uh, save those things and treasure them . . ."

"Save them?" I asked.

"Yes," the man said.

"She doesn't want Richard to have that necklace?" I asked. He had given it to her as a special gift.

"Uh, she said something—there was some special jewelry in her room she said. I forgot what—it might have been that necklace. But uh, yeah, go—go ahead, but the rest of her stuff is irre—is irrelevant," he stuttered.

"Okay."

"She felt sure that ya'll would divvy up. And . . ."

"What about her high school ring?" I asked. It had not been on her when her body was found, and Mom and Dad wanted it to keep.

"Uh, that's—she said everything else would be decided by the family." He seemed to be making it up as he went along.

"But Shari was—was not afraid, and she didn't cry or anything?" I was reaching for hope.

"No, she didn't do anything," he stated firmly. "And, uh, you can handle it if I tell you how she died?"

One minute he seemed sorry and repentant, and now he cruelly wanted to hurt me. *Can I handle it?* I asked myself. I quietly said, "Yes."

"Okay, now be strong." He seemed to be enjoying this. "She said she—you were. She told me all about the family and everything. We talked and—oh God," he stammered, "and I am a family friend. That's the sad part."

Somehow I didn't believe him. No friend of ours would do what he'd done. "You are a family friend?"

"Yeah," he almost seemed to laugh, "and that's why I can't face ya'll. You—you'll find out in the morning or tomorrow, but, uh, forgive me and, uh, Dawn, uh, Shari—I don't know whether you were aware of . . ." He began telling me awful things he claimed he'd done to Shari. As he reeled off the physical and sexual abuses, I could only bite my lip and pray they were all lies. He bragged about how he'd tied her to the bedpost and then proceeded to suffocate her. Tears welled up in my eyes. How could the sheriff expect me to stay on the phone and listen to this?

"I was unaware she had the disease," he continued. "I probably wouldn't ever taken her. And, uh, I shouldn't have took her anyway. It just got out of hand."

"Uh-uh," was all I could say. I was stunned.

"And, uh, I'd asked her out before, and she said she would if she wasn't going with anybody."

"Uh-uh." I knew he was lying.

"And, uh, she said that, uh—oh, yeah, make sure Charlie Keyes—you know him? The reporter on WIS?"

"I can't think of who he is right now."

"Okay, they'll know who he is. He's the one that wears the bow tie on Channel 10." All of a sudden it registered. "He's the head news fellow on this case for Channel 10. Tell him to be sure to get in touch with Ann Davis because—"

"Ann Davis?" I asked, as I was continuing to write.

"Yeah," he answered. "She's probably already told him some information. I had to use them for mediums because they were tapping your house and stuff. And I know the ironic part—I had to see what was going on at the house—at your house."

"Yes." I wondered what he was getting at, almost afraid to hear what was next.

"And I was there Saturday morning for the search," he mocked.

"You were at the search Saturday?" I couldn't believe what I was hearing. The person who was responsible for my sister's death during the early hours of that morning actually had the audacity to show up at our house to search among so many friends and family?

"Yes, I was," he boasted. "And if—oh God, Dawn. I wish, uh, I wish ya'll could help me, but it's just too late."

"Let me tell you something, okay?" I fumbled for words to calm him down. "God can forgive you."

"Well, I have to go now, Dawn. I know the—"

"And through God, we can forgive you also."

"Well, uh, Dawn—will you forgive me then?" He seemed sincere.

"Yes," I said, and I meant it. Although I had felt hate for this man earlier, somehow I knew that I could forgive him with God's strength. Only God could have changed my heart.

"Your family?" he asked. That was another question. "But I—I just—it—it's—I'll have to take the other choice that—that Shari Faye said to me. I just can't live with myself like this. I'm not . . ." He was beginning to whine again.

"You just need to think about that a little harder—"

"I'm not going to be caged up like a dog," he said, full of self-pity. "Okay, now, is there any other questions—short. I've got to go now. Time's running out . . ."

"Uh, when—when you killed Shari," I could hardly get those words out, "was she at peace? She wasn't afraid or anything?"

"She was not," he said. Why was I even listening to him when he was probably just making all this up? "She was at peace. She knew that God was with her, and she was going to become an angel."

"And—and she wrote that letter to us of her own free will and all that was—"

"She sure did," he seemed proud to say, in his thick southern accent. "Everything I've told ya'll has been the truth. It—hasn't everything come true?"

"Yes, it has."

"Okay, and now, I'll be in the area, uh, from—just a long enough time to set this up for myself . . ."

"Uh-uh." I was trying to keep him going, but surely they'd been able to trace the call by now. How much longer did this have to go on?

". . . and, uh, like I said, I—also Charlie and everything requested, I mean, I told you that I requested Shari—I asked

Shari Faye if I could do this, and she said it was fine with her to have the minister—the preacher from Lexington Baptist be in the ambulance."

"Be in the ambulance," I read back to him. "Lewis Abbott?" I asked, referring to our pastor.

"The one that's going to do the funeral Saturday?"

"Yes." I was becoming more aggravated with him.

"Okay."

"Can—can I ask you one more question?"

"One more and that's it," he demanded.

"When—when you, uh, you told us that you—Shari was kidnapped at gunpoint?" I could not understand why she ever got into that car, gun or no gun. Dad had always taught us to run, no matter what.

"Yeah?" He seemed uninterested.

"But she knew you?" I hoped that might get him talking again.

"Yeah. At first, see, I pulled up and, uh, I'm telling you the truth. I have no reason to lie to ya'll."

"Right."

"Okay. And, uh, I had her—asked her to stand there and I took two pictures," he said.

"You asked her to stand where?"

"At the mailbox with her car in the background." He seemed to think I was an idiot by his tone of voice. "Those pictures—detailed pictures will be with—with the letter that you receive probably—since I'm out of town, probably not 'til Saturday."

"Uh-uh." My hand was beginning to cramp from all the notes I'd taken.

"And Charlie Keyes will get a copy and your family will

get a copy and it's addressed to you unless the mail holds it up."

"So she didn't realize that you were fixing to kidnap her?"

"That's exactly right." He seemed pleased with himself.

"Okay."

"Shari told me—Shari Faye told me—remember I told you on the fifth day to let them know where she was so her blessings of the body could be blessed, right?"

I was lost. "Why on the fifth day did she want us to find her?" My anger was rising quickly. "Why not—"

"I don't know." His was too. "She just—she just said that. I don't know. I don't have any idea. I'm telling you exactly how she died, so she died of suffocation. And so, you know, the—okay, anything else?"

He was truly enjoying this. My anger would not subside now. "Why did you—why did you do that?" I practically shouted at him.

"She—I gave her a choice. I—to shoot her or give her a drug overdose or suffocate her," he said, as if it were an everyday normal activity.

I could only choke out, "Why did you have to kill her?"

"It got out of hand." He sounded as if he expected me to understand. "I got scared because, ah, only God knows, Dawn. I don't know why. God forgive me for this. I hope and I got to straighten it out, or He'll and I'll be there the rest of my life, but I'm not going to be in prison and electric chair."

"But I don't think taking your life is the answer to this. Or—"

"I'll . . . I'll think . . ."

"Or to forgive you." I didn't even know if I was making sense anymore.

"I'll think about it. Well, Dawn, I've got to go now," he said, and I was ready for him to go. "It's been too long and, ah, tell them to just forget about the search. I'll be in the area long enough in the morning for them to, ah, find me and by the time I call, ah, there, Charlie Keyes will know exactly the setup."

"Well, . . ." I didn't know what to say.

"I hope now, ah, I know why I'm staying on the phone, all right, they are taping this. I don't want anything messed up, okay?"

"Okay," I said, wondering how things could possibly be anymore messed up than they already were.

"They are taping it, right?"

"Uh-uh," I said honestly, not caring that he knew anymore. I was ready for this conversation to end. Why hadn't the police gotten him by now? We had been on for a long time now.

"Okay, good. Okay and anything else?"

"Uh, I, uh, just, ah . . ." I was tired and couldn't think of anything to ask or say.

"Oh, yeah, let me tell you. The other night they almost caught me," he said with a dry laugh in his voice. "I wanted them to catch me. I felt that way all that time, but now—"

"When . . . when was this?"

"Ah, when I called at 9:45."

"When you were over near Jake's Landing?"

"Yeah, I was at that Fast Fare thing," he answered.

"Yeah." I remembered.

"I pulled out twenty yards in front of two flashing lights—"

"What color car did you have?" I asked, as the question was passed to me on a note.

"They hit it dead on it, red, and they didn't even, Dawn, I

88

can't get over this." He laughed again. "They didn't even turn around and follow me, and I cut right at that blinking light down there to go the back way on Old Cherokee Road."

"Ah . . ." I was dumbfounded.

"And there was a highway patrolman or somebody in front of me and pulled the car in front of me and let me turn right on Old Cherokee Road. Can you believe it?" He seemed so pleased with his accomplishment.

"So you really wanted to be caught?" I asked.

"At that time, but it's too late now."

"What kind of car was it?"

"Oh, well, they were mighty close. I, Dawn, they're not going to catch me, and I, I can't give you much information because I got to make it back in time, and they'll stop me before I get back if I tell you, but they're right, it was a red one, and I almost got caught three or four times."

"Was it a red Jetta?" I probed.

"Dawn, that's irrelevant now. If I die now or if I die at 6:00 in the morning, it's irrelevant. Well, listen, ah, Dawn—"

"I really, I wish you would—"

"Anything else?" He didn't seem to hear me.

"I wish you would not kill yourself," I finished.

"And she told me to tell you, please go back to Carowinds. I know you live in Charlotte, and, ah, I know a lot about your family, and, ah, go back and start singing and give it your best and that she knows that she'll be singing like crazy. She was, ah, when she said that, she was smiling. She'll be singing like crazy."

"She was smiling?" I asked, hoping against hope that Shari really did say those things and wondering how he could have known them if she hadn't.

"She was smiling, and, well . . ."

"So, she wasn't afraid the whole time?" I couldn't understand it, even as strong a person as Shari was. I needed to know.

"No, never," he affirmed again.

"Because she knew that she was going to be with God?"

"That's exactly right, the whole time, the whole time," he repeated. "She's so strong-willed and, and—"

"But I just really, I wish you would think about not killing yourself," I interrupted.

"I will, Dawn."

"You need to think about it a lot because . . ."

"Okay, well, put it this way, if I, if I decide between now and I call the sheriff, he'll know, with Charlie Keyes, 6:00 in the morning, I'll, ah, oh, I'll . . ."

He seemed to be panicking again, so I tried to calm him again by saying, "Listen, our prayers will be for you."

"Okay," he said with finality in his voice. "I'll call you collect."

"Did you hear what I said?" I was tiring of his subject changing.

"Will you be home tonight?"

"We, we are home tonight," I assured him. "Can I ask you, listen, our prayers will be with you, okay? God can do anything, and He can forgive you for this."

"Yeah, but you know what's going to happen to me, Dawn? I'm going to be fried."

Not that again, I thought. "You don't know that. God can work miracles. You don't know that that'll happen to you . . ."

"Well, Dawn . . ."

"God is merciful no matter what we do." I was running out of things to say to persuade him.

"It's time now, it's time." He seemed to be ready to hang up. "I got to go now and I'll just, I'll think about it, but I've got a lot of things on my mind now. I know you know that, right?"

"Right." He seemed to be hanging on every word I said now, dependent on my agreeing with him.

"And, ah, ah, you answer the phone every time it rings tonight."

"Me answer the phone tonight every time it rings?"

"That's right and if it's collect, and I'll say from the break of day, you'll know." He seemed to think his little password was so clever, the break of day meaning Dawn.

"If we're asleep, you let it keep ringing, okay?"

"I will, I will." He seemed to like thinking that he was in control. "Okay, well, God bless all of us."

"God bless you, too."

"And . . ."

Mom was walking directly over to me, reaching her hand out for the phone. "Wait, Mother wants to say something to you."

"Please—"

"Listen," I interrupted, "Mom wants to say something to you."

"All right," he said nervously, "just one thing and then I'm gone."

I handed the receiver to Mom.

"Hello," she began.

"Yes."

"Ah, . . ." She looked as if she couldn't believe she was talking to the animal that had so cruelly taken her daughter's life.

"Well, hurry," he rudely demanded. "Just say one thing and that's it. Dawn will tell you and you listen to the recordings, and there will be a letter you'll receive probably the next day with pictures and detailed information from the time I picked Shari up at the mailbox until tonight and my departure from this earth. It's over. I will not be taken alive. Dawn told me to turn myself in or turn myself over to God or I'll never live in peace and never be forgiven and go to Heaven."

"Well," Mom said, groping for control, "turn yourself over to God. That's most important."

"I am and this is the only way. I'm not going to spend my life in prison and go to the electric chair," he sobbed.

"Ah—"

"Well," he interrupted, "ah, Dawn knows everything and, ah, God bless all of us and I hope—"

"Listen, I want to ask you something."

"This just got out of hand." He seemed to know already what she was going to ask. "This got out of hand . . ."

"All you had to do was let her go."

"I was scared." He seemed to be begging my mother to understand. "She, she, she was dehydrating so bad."

"You could have called me for medicine." Mom was crying now. "I would have met you anywhere."

"Well, that's irrelevant now."

"Oh," she cried, "I mean all you had to do was let her go. Such a beautiful young life."

"I know that. That's why I have to join her now, hopefully, and, ah, Mrs. Smith, please, ah, please, uh, uh, okay, well, that's it." He was losing control. "I got to go."

"Did she know you when you stopped her?"

"Yeah, ah, there'll be pictures and I took pic . . . two pictures Instamatic of, I made her stand . . . well, before she knew I was going to kidnap her, I asked her to stand at the mailbox and you'll see by the picture, her car door and cars in the background, and, ah, there will be pictures all, I think there's about eight pictures and Charlie Keyes will be receiving a set and a detailed letter, like I told you, at his house and I, if it's, if this mail doesn't slow it down, which it probably will, if you don't get it tomorrow, you'll get it the next day. You'll get exact copies, the pictures that he gets and, ah, exact letters, too."

"Do you know all of us or just Shari?" she asked, trembling, still intent on getting some answers.

"I know the whole family unfortunately," he began. "That's why I can't face you. Okay, well, Mrs. Smith, please, ah, if I decide different, I've already told Dawn what's going to happen. Her answer the phone tonight only and it will be collect and I'm going to allow myself enough time, just enough time to get back in the area to set everything up if you don't hear from me tonight, and Sheriff Metts and Charlie Keyes . . . I used him as a medium today, because I knew the calls were being traced, and they came real close to catching me three or four different times and they were correct—I am in a red vehicle."

"What kind?" Mom asked.

"I'm sorry, I don't want them to catch me before I meet my Maker on judgment day."

"You think the Maker's going to forgive you now?" Mom mocked angrily.

"He'll, He'll do that or I'll be crucified and go to Hell," he said, the fear evident in his voice.

"That's right."

"Well . . ."

"And you need to meet with somebody who can talk to you," Mom tried to encourage him, forcing her tone to change.

"Well, I'm, I've got a lot to think about and I'm, I'm gone, Mrs. Smith, and, ah, please, I," he stuttered, sounding very emotional, "I know this might be selfish, but, ah, you all please, ask a special prayer for me? Your, your daughter said that she was not afraid and she was strong-willed. She, ah, knew that she was going to Heaven, was going to be an angel and like I told Dawn, she was going to be singing like crazy and—"

"Did she . . ." Emotion cut off my mother's voice at the thought of her daughter's words.

"When she said that, she was smiling." He seemed to be trying to comfort her.

"Did you tell her you were going to kill her?" Mom's voice was now full of all the pain, grief, and fear of what her daughter had gone through.

"Yes, I did and I gave her the choice, like, it's on the recording. I asked her if she wanted to be drug overdose, shot, or, ah, suffocated, and she picked the suffocation," he cruelly repeated.

"My God, how could you?" Mom sobbed as her voice broke with unbearable grief and horror.

"Well, forgive us. God, God . . ."

"Not us, you."

"God only knows why this happened," he tried to explain. "I don't know. It just got out of hand."

"That's . . . I thought, you know what?"

"Good-bye, Mrs. Smith."

"I thought you were considerate and loving and a kind

person," she accused, tears streaming down her tired, strained face. There was no reply. He was gone.

10

I STARED AT THE PHONE. MOM WAS CRYING AS DAD TOOK HER back to their bedroom. Robert stood by the doorway, his face full of worry and concern. It was after 9:00 P.M., and I was emotionally exhausted. I didn't think I could endure another conversation with this maniac. Not only had he killed my sister, but he continued to cause more pain and fear by calling and taunting us. How much longer could this go on?

The call was traced to a phone booth at the Grand Central Truck Stop at I-77 and Highway 200 in Great Falls, SC. For someone who claimed he wanted to be caught, the killer was going to a lot of trouble to make sure he wasn't. Had he driven out of town for the sole purpose of calling me? The FBI felt that he had no intention of surrendering, since he had craftily withheld the location of Shari's body until decomposition had practically destroyed forensic evidence. They feared he'd strike again.

We later learned that, in fact, the killer did call Channel 10's reporter, Charlie Keyes, and had given Keyes the same information he gave us.

As I made my way into the hallway and turned to go up the stairs, I found Robert sitting on the bottom step, his face showing traces of tears. I sat down beside him and put my arm around his skinny shoulders.

"I hate him," he whispered hoarsely. "I hate him for killing Shari. I could kill him myself. I hate . . ." his voice broke as he turned toward the window.

"Robert, don't say that," I begged. "You don't mean what you're saying." But as I looked into his greenish-brown eyes, I saw that he did, and I hated what was happening to him. Had this monster turned my gentle brother into a hardened, angry person? All I could do was hold Robert and cry, too. I remembered how we used to bicker as children, the usual "two-against-one" arguments that always ended with Robert being left out. How stupid it all seemed now. He was the most precious little brother in the whole world, and I wanted to make sure he knew that. *No little brother should have to go through what he's been through,* I thought, as I held him in my trembling arms. He was so sensitive to others. He loved Jesus. The other boys his age cared nothing about the things of God, but Robert had a quiet time with the Lord every night before he went to sleep.

Robert was a precious gift to me from the Lord. We'd both lost a sister, but I still had Robert. I promised the Lord that night that although in some ways I'd let Shari down, I would do my best to be the Christian older sister my little brother needed . . . an example, a shoulder to cry on, an encourager and cheerleader in all he did, but most of all, a friend.

●

I awoke from the first decent night's sleep I'd had since it all began. As soon as my eyes opened, I knew what today would hold. Mom had decided to put the funeral off for three days until Shari's friends and classmates would be back from their cruise. The time had come.

The house was unusually quiet, and the mood somber. As I quietly showered and got ready, I prayed for each member of my family—Mom, Dad, Robert, Nana, and all of our aunts, uncles, and cousins who would be present. I lifted a special prayer for Richard. His love for Shari had been so great that he seemed like part of the family. I wondered how he would handle today and asked for special grace and strength for us all.

I made my way downstairs, tiptoeing for some reason, and I found everyone ready, just waiting until it was time to go. Through the front windows of the dining area, I saw the black cars coming down the long driveway. I took in a deep breath. No longer did it seem a bad dream; now I knew too well it was reality. I hoped I was ready for this day. With a prayer in my heart, I walked to the car. We rode in silence, just as on the way to pick out the casket. But this time Shari would be in it. Not really, I kept telling myself. It's just her empty body, but it was the body of the sister I had loved so much, that I had watched grow up and shared so much of my life with. Oh, how I needed strength other than my own. *"I can do all things through Christ who strengthens me,"* I continued to tell myself. *I am not alone.*

As we pulled up to the church, I saw cars parked everywhere. Mom looked as if she were about to faint when the pallbearers lifted the casket out of the back of the hearse. I held onto her, finding no words to say. She was weeping uncontrollably, and I, too, could not contain my tears. *I have to get myself together,* I kept telling myself, *before I walk in that door.* The precious, destroyed body of my sister now in front of us, we began to follow the young men who carried the casket into the church. They, too, were weeping. I hated for them to have to do this, and I wanted to tell them how sorry I was.

As we passed slowly to the front pew of the Lexington Baptist Church, I couldn't bring myself to raise my eyes to anyone, although I could tell the church was completely full. I could only focus on the pew where my quivering legs were taking me, where I could quit walking and sit, so that no one could see my face any longer. I could no longer hold back the tears when I saw the shiny, silver casket before me. I wanted to run up to it, wrap my arms around it, and tell Shari how much I loved her, how much I missed her, and how I hated what she had been through. Instead I sat motionless as a statue, holding tightly to Robert's hand.

"As friends and loved ones and a concerned community, we've come here today with a broken heart, with a sense of grief, of awe, and of fear," our pastor, Lewis Abbott began. Tears continued to stream down my cheeks as I stared straight ahead at his grief-stricken face. "We have become united as a community as we realize the frailty of life and the necessity of support one for another. . . . I want to say a brief word about suffering and the understanding of this occasion in our life together, as a family and as a community.

"I would first say a word to you, Bob, and Hilda, Dawn, and Robert," he continued, "and the rest of these family and friends gathered here, that there is not an answer for you to the question of why. And the asking of that question delays a great deal the ministry the Lord can have in your hearts, because why is not the question that rests before us. The question that lies before us is what meaning can this have in our lives, how can God use it to bless others, and do we really believe what we say we believe? All of us must suffer, and if we believe in the Lord Jesus, we must not blame God. God does not do what has been done here. It is because of the confusion and the sin and depravity of man that we come to an occasion like this. And I am grateful to tell you that we've come here today to celebrate real life, not death. Grieved and broken . . . shattered, yes, but for Shari this is not an end; it is the beginning. And we are committed to that. And I encourage you to allow the Lord to do supernaturally what no one else can do for you. Let us pray: Merciful God, thank You for being God, and thank You for taking the pieces of life and putting them together in the person of the Lord Jesus. Thank You for the resurrection, for hope . . ."

Pastor Abbott made his way back to his chair, and then the congregation sang. The words of "A Mighty Fortress Is Our God" just washed over me, and I felt a peace I could not explain. I knew it was the presence of God in my heart. As the beautiful verse from Isaiah was read, "Fear thou not, I am with thee. Be not dismayed for I am thy God. I will strengthen thee, yea, I will help thee, and I will uphold you with the right hand of My goodness," I looked down the pew to see my family's reaction. My mother and father seemed to be lost within themselves. Robert and I continued to hold hands. As I glanced over at him, I noticed how handsome he looked in his coat and tie, but his face made my heart ache. This was so much for a boy his age to endure.

Ray Ridgeway, a pastor and special friend to our family, continued, "It was nearly twenty years ago that word spread fast around our vast globe with a name of a little-known coal mining town of Abberfan Wells. In that small Welsh village for many years as the coal miners would come out of the mines each day, they would bring what they called the slag, which was the waste from the mines. And they would pile it on a hill just north of town. The hill grew through the months and through the years, and gradually the hill became a small mountain. One particular day after the spring rains had come for several days, in an instant of time, the mountain gave way, and in a few moments more than one hundred children in the school had been killed beneath the slag heap. Reporters from all over the world went to Abberfan to get the story. As the friends, the neighbors, and the families came to look for their loved ones, the reporters stood by, and one American reporter said, 'I cannot believe in God after seeing this.' A Welsh father, looking for his son, stood there a moment and leaned on his shovel. He laid it down, went over to the reporter, touched him on his arm, and he said, 'Friend, the God I know is here weeping with us. Don't ever forget one day He lost His child, too.' And I believe today our God is here weeping with us. Our God is here, He cares, He understands."

Rev. Graham Lyons then spoke of living near us as neighbors. He had seen Shari grow up. He had seen her give her life to Christ. And he and his wife had come to Christ partly, he said, because of the way our entire family had shown Christ in our lives. Then he voiced our hope of seeing Shari again, of looking forward to being with her in that place Jesus has prepared, where there are no tears, pain, or death.

As we stood to our feet for the final hymn, my feet felt numb from not moving during the entire service. Then the words of "Amazing Grace," which I'd probably sung a hundred times, seemed more precious than ever before—"ten thousand years, bright shining as the sun; we've no less days to sing God's praise." Shari had begun to sing it.

The pianist continued to play the sweet melody while we made our way out of the auditorium to go to Lexington Memorial Cemetery. Through the pain, I felt an incredible presence, as though the very presence of God was with us. Yet as we walked to our car, sudden fear came over me—fear that the man who killed my sister could be there, waiting for us, to gawk at or harm us. The SLED agents staying right by our sides reminded us of possible danger. But our entire family was protected, and officers were everywhere in the crowd. It infuriated me that this man had done this to us—that we could not forget our fear even at the time of our great grief and pain.

Through the tinted window of the limousine, I could see pink ribbons in honor of Shari everywhere—on car antennas, mailboxes, doors, and even on street signs. Slowly we made our way through the unbearable heat. I wondered where he was—the man who had done this awful deed. Would he be there among the mourners? Was he actually sorry for what he'd done, or was he somewhere out of sight, smirking?

Everyone from the church must have come to the burial service. There must have been a thousand people there. We were making our way back to the cars when someone in the crowd began to shout, "I'm sorry, I'm really sorry." Deadly silence followed, and then panic broke out. My first thought was, *Oh, God, he is here! That is him. He is confessing right here in front of everyone!* One of Shari's friends fell to the ground, shrieking that the man was coming to get her. The terror in her voice triggered hysterical outbursts from other women around her. Chaos ensued.

"Whoever is responsible for this, I believe you're here. I love you and will not hurt you. Come forward right now. There's no bitterness or hatred." The announcement came from the dark figure of a man standing in an evangelical pose with arms outstretched against the sun's hazy glare. I could not make out who it was.

Agents whisked us into the cars and quickly drove us away from the cemetery. I saw Sheriff Metts grab the man by the arm and lead him to a patrol car. The tinted windows cut down the glare, and I couldn't believe what I was seeing. It was a member of our church. Had he been the one who had taken Shari's life so cruelly? So we did, in fact, know him? Was his the voice I'd grown to dread? I couldn't believe it. This man in his thirties had always hung out with the kids in the youth group. We'd all taken him in under our wings, to make him feel special and part of the group. Once again that suspicion of everyone arose. But later we learned that this man was just trying to show his concern, thinking that if he made an appeal, the killer might give himself up. This friend was such a compassionate person, always trying to help others. I felt foolish that I'd suspected him even for a moment. Well, then, if that was a false alarm, had the killer actually been there? Had he heard our friend's plea and fled in fear?

11

I HAD NO MORE THAN CHANGED MY CLOTHES AND FLOPPED down across the bed when the phone rang. I jumped back up immediately and ran down the stairs in my stocking feet to get it. Surely it wouldn't be him—not today, not now.

"Hello."

"I have a collect call for Dawn Smith from Shari. Will you pay for the call?" came the operator's voice.

"From whom?" I said, irritated at his insensitivity.

"Shari," she repeated.

"Yes." I sighed.

"Go ahead, please," the operator told him.

"Dawn, like the break of day," came the ugly voice.

"What?" I didn't want to play games; my emotions were shot.

"Like the break of day," he repeated.

"Like the break of day," I wearily muttered.

"Uh-uh." He seemed to be pleased with his little code.

"Uh-uh."

"Ah, Dawn, I'm real afraid now and everything . . ." he said.

I didn't believe him. "Uh-uh."

"And I have to, ah, make a decision," he went on. "I'm

going to stay in this area until God gives me the strength to decide which way, and I did go to the funeral today."

"You did?" The shock was evident in my voice.

"Yes, and, ah, that ignorant policeman—he directed me into a parking space. Fellow, blue uniform outside, and they were taking license plate numbers down and stuff. Please tell Sheriff Metts I'm not jerking anybody around; I'm not playing games; this is reality and I'm not an idiot. When he finds out my background, he'll see I'm a highly intelligent person."

"Uh-uh." I had to keep him talking even if it was the day of my sister's funeral.

"Okay, and I want to fill in some gaps here because between now and next Saturday, the anniversary date of Shari Faye . . ." He paused.

"Yeah?"

"I'm going to do one way or the other, or if God gives me the strength before then, ever when and I'll call you and give you . . . all I'll say is—"

"Between now and next Saturday?" I interrupted.

"Yes."

"I think you need to make a decision before then," I angrily said. I couldn't imagine waiting an entire week for him to put us off again.

"Well, now listen carefully; don't ask questions. Think of questions you want but not now, okay . . . and I'll code so you know it won't be a hoax. I don't want . . . I never wanted that. Okay, we'll still use, when you answer the phone or whoever, I'll say, Dawn, like the break of day."

"Okay," I said as I was writing.

"We'll only know that, okay?"

"Okay," I assured him.

"All right, and, ah, I could tell her casket was closed, but did ya'll honor Shari's request for folding her hands?" he asked.

"Yes, yes, we did, of course." I wanted to scream at him.

"Okay, she'll, she'll like that. That'll please her. Okay and, ah, tell Sheriff Metts, the FBI, that's like the fear of God in you for sure. They treat this like Bonnie and Clyde. They go out and gun you down, and if I decide, if God gives me the strength to just surrender like that, I'll call you and all I'll do, like I said, Shari Faye's location and, ah, when I see them drive up, and I'll see Charlie Keyes and Sheriff Metts get out of the car, they'll recognize me. I'll approach them, and I'll put my hands straight up in the air and turn my back to them, and they can approach me without shooting me and stuff, all right?"

"Okay."

"Okay, now listen carefully, now, Shari Faye was, ah, I'm trying to fill in all the gaps here. Shari Faye was, ah, God accepted her in Lexington County at 4:58 in the morning and—"

"You're—" I interrupted.

"I delivered her to Saluda County, and also I told you exactly, I have no reason to lie to you. I told you exactly how she died and so forth, and when I took the duct tape off of her, they, they, the examiner said they're having problems telling how she died . . ."

"Uh-uh." What did it matter now? How could he talk like this was just an everyday event? My stomach knotted.

"Ah, when I took the duct tape off, it took a lot of hair with it, and so that'll help 'em out," he said.

"Okay." I barely responded, aching for my sister and not

wanting to hear one more minute of what he'd done to her again. Hadn't the call been traced yet?

"Well, hold on a minute now and let's see . . ." I heard the sound of a passing car wherever he was—evidently at another pay phone.

"Where's the duct tape?" I thought to ask.

"Huh?" he asked, thrown by my question. "Only God knows, I don't . . . okay, okay, now listen, now Richard, ah, okay, did you receive the thing and the pictures in the mail?" He sounded nervous.

"They're coming," I said, fearing his possible anger. We had not received anything.

"They . . . it's what . . . the FBI going to intercept them . . . okay, it's written to you. I got Shari Faye to address three or four different things," he explained.

"Uh-uh," hope rising in my voice at the thought of receiving something else with Shari's handwriting on it.

"And it's written to you in her handwriting."

"Was it written to me?" I choked.

"It's addressed to you," he began. "Okay, and now, she, she gave me your address in Charlotte, and there's one picture she wanted me to send to you, and you'll get that in about a week or so, to your Charlotte address, and it's, this little note is for your eyes only in her handwriting, and she said— Richard—don't tell him this, it'll break his heart. She was getting ready to break up with him because he was jealous and that, ah, she couldn't go anywhere and talk to any fellows without him arguing with her and . . ."

"Yes?"

"And every time he'd come down to the flea market, she worked in the concession stand."

"Yeah."

"She, he'd get mad because she couldn't talk to him and working, ah, he worked at the Casual Corner at the Point, I believe," he said.

"Uh-uh," I agreed. That was where Richard worked. Did Shari really tell him all this? But she was head over heels in love with Richard. The man had to be making up the part about Shari breaking up with Richard, but I didn't know how to tell what was truth and what was fiction.

"Okay, and let's see, and there's only me involved in this, okay, and we talked, ah, from actually she wrote the last will and testament, will and testament 3:12 A.M." He seemed to be reading from notes again. "She kind of joked and said, 'They won't mind if I round it off to 3:10.'"

"Right," I said. That was so like Shari.

"So from 2:00 in the morning from the time she actually knew until she died at 4:58, we talked a lot and everything, and she picked the time. She said she was ready to depart. God was ready to accept her as an angel . . ."

"You told her that she was going to die, is that right?"

"Yeah," he answered, "okay, and, ah, all those times and stuff I gave you before were correct and accurate. When are you going back to Charlotte and get the letter?" I was afraid of his question. "It's, well, it's going to be whenever I get the strength and God shows me which way, I'll mail it like a couple of hours before."

He was not making much sense to me, but I didn't want him asking me any more questions about myself. I hadn't even thought about when or if I would be going back to Charlotte, but I certainly did not want him to know. "Okay, where is Shari's high school ring?" I asked, thinking quickly.

109

"Ah, Shari's high school ring was not with her."

"It wasn't with her?" I didn't believe him. She never went anywhere without it.

"No, not unless it was in her car or her pocketbook."

"She always wears that ring, and if it was, please," I pleaded.

"I'm telling you the truth," he insisted.

"The family would really like to have it," I pressed.

"I'm returning everything," he insisted again. "I mean, I don't have anything of Shari's. I don't have that."

"Ah." I didn't know what to say.

"Okay, and she told me in that thing, ah, for your eyes only, and she said something very personal about you, also, that, and she wanted me to tell you this . . ." Just when I was expecting some word from Shari, anything at all, my heart stopped as he all of a sudden began to talk of crude things concerning my sister. He was obviously enjoying himself. "I made clip notes afterwards. I couldn't remember everything, and she said she wanted to get clo . . . I don't know why she said that, ah, and, ah, she said to tell Robert, Jr.—that's the brother, right? Your brother?"

"Yeah." I was afraid of what he was going to say.

"Okay, tell him to grow up and meet his goals and pick a sport out, and he's a big boy, and, ah, excel in it, but with religious attitude that, ah, winning is not everything." I felt his words could have been a message from Shari to Robert. Would I ever know? He continued, "And your father and mother, tell them to please just discontinue, ah, helping people that, from R. Richards, ever what that is and the chaplain at the jail and turn their spare energies into helping, ah, orphans in the U.S., in our, well, in your area, in your local area."

110

"Uh-uh," I said, trying to understand what he was refer-ring to. John G. Richards Home was a juvenile delinquent home for boys where my father had had a ministry for several years.

"Okay," he continued, "and then the last thing, oh yeah, for respect of your family, Shari Faye always told me to respect the family, and I didn't mail Charlie Keyes a set of pictures and letters. I want your family only. So when you find me, uh, if God gives me the strength, ever which way He decides, it'll be in a plastic bag on my body, on my person and it, I'll, I'll mark out, I'll cut out certain portions of pictures where you'll know it's the real thing, because that's the only set of the Instamatic pictures and the letter and I'll burn everything else with ashes, and it'll be in a plastic bag because if the medium got a hold of this, they'll have a field day, and the reason I chose Charlie Keyes as a medium, because I thought he was very level-headed and he wouldn't let it get out of hand."

"Uh-uh." I was dumbfounded.

"And, okay, I can trust him, because I kind of know him," he lied. "Okay, ah, the last thing she said is, ah, something, things that I went back and made clip notes so that I could remember. A song, she wouldn't tell me, she said, well, I have to keep some things secret with you, and she kind of chuckled."

"Uh-uh." My mind was racing to make some kind of sense out of all this.

"She said that Dawn would know on her birthday, which is what, June the twelfth or something?" he asked.

"On Shari's?" I asked, confused.

"I mean Shari's."

"Her birthday?" I asked again.

"Yeah," he answered, "June or Au . . . she told me . . ."

"It's June," I confirmed.

"Okay, well, ever when it is, on that date or it might be today, no, no, it's not . . . I think she said the twelfth or something," he seemed to be trying to remember something, "but anyway, ah, she said to pick her favorite song and just you and the family, ah, you sing it out, ah, she'll be listening, and, ah, put some real feelings behind it. Okay, and let's see, let me go back through it. Okay, I was at the search Saturday morning and also Tuesday morning I showed up when they called the volunteers off—"

"You were there . . ." I couldn't finish, gasping at the thought of him being so near.

"Yeah." He laughed. "And I was there for the funeral this morning. They took license numbers; still, I'm not an idiot. I never had any problems before, and it's just something that got out of hand and that's all."

Murdering my sister was just something that got out of hand? Fury boiled within me. "Can I ask you something?"

"Okay, now ask questions, but hurry."

"Ah, I know that you keep telling me that you're telling me the truth, but, ah, you did tell me that you would give yourself up at 6:00 that morning," I began.

"Yeah, I—"

"Well, what happened?" I mocked.

"I didn't have the strength."

"What?" I was sick of him and his wimpy games.

"I didn't have the strength," he said again, breathing heavily. "I was scared. I can't even hardly read my handwriting."

"Well, listen—" I tried to sound sympathetic and soothing.

"Hurry, I've got to go."

"No matter what you've done, you know that Christ died for you so that you could be forgiven."

"I know that," he whimpered.

"And, and, if you would give yourself up—"

"Do you know what would happen, Dawn?" he blurted out. "Do you realize yet, ah, Sheriff Metts—"

"Do YOU realize what happened . . ." I was sick of him worrying about himself after what he'd done to my sister and family.

"Sheriff Metts would give me help for a couple of months, and then they'd find out I'm sane, and then I'd get tried and get sent to the electric chair, put in prison the rest of my life." His voice was high with panic. "I'm not going to stay in prison the rest of my life. I'm not going to, ah . . ."

"But, if you—"

"Go the electric chair," he finished.

"Don't you realize what you've put us through? How could you think about what would happen to yourself?"

"Okay, any other questions?" He was trying to change the subject. "I've filled in all the holes and everything. Anything else?"

"Ah . . ."

"If the only reason you wouldn't get that letter today or probably Monday is that the FBI intercepted it," he fumbled.

Captain Gasque handed me a note that said, "Ring?"

"Can you tell me where her ring is? You really don't know where it is?"

"No, I don't, Dawn. I would send it to you if I did. I have no reason, I'm not asking money, materialistic things; I don't have any reason for, her. She was not wearing a high school ring when she got in the car."

"Ah . . . can you tell me . . ."

"So maybe she left it at the pool party she came from," he suggested.

Captain Gasque passed me another note. I read it aloud, "Where did Shari die?"

"I told you, 4:58 in the morning."

"No, I know the time. Where?"

"Saturday morning in, ah, Lexington County," he answered.

"In Lexington County?"

"Uh-uh."

"Where?" I persisted.

"Anything else you want to ask me? Hurry now." He was trying to change the subject again and talking quickly.

"That's what I'm asking you—where?"

"Ah, anything else?"

"You won't answer that for me?" I demanded.

"No."

"You said anything I'd ask, you'd tell me."

"Okay, I'll tell you. Ah, number one, I don't know exactly the location, but, number one, ah, right, right on Highway 1. I don't know the name of the highway, 391 or something like that, but right next to the Saluda County line. That's all I can tell you. Okay, anything else? I'm getting ready to go."

"Ah . . ."

"At 4:58 in the morning, set your alarm wherever you are, and I'll call you and, ah, exactly what God made up His mind and tell Sheriff Metts that—"

"Wait," I interrupted, "now what?"

"Hold on a minute." He was obviously trying to find his place in his notes again. "4:58 in the morning . . ."

"Hello?" I tried to hear over the noise that was coming from his end.

"Yes," he answered.

"Okay, 4:58." I tried to get him back on track.

"In the morning," he finished.

"This morning?"

"No, next Saturday."

"Next Saturday?" I asked. I could not accept that he could possibly put off his surrender or suicide or whatever he was talking about for another week while we helplessly sat by, waiting.

"Yeah, on the anniversary date. Okay, I'll call you and tell you the exact location," he was saying. "All I do is—"

"Listen," I interrupted.

"Just like I did Shari Faye's."

"I can't believe this because you've not been telling me the truth." I was angry, and didn't care if he knew it.

"Okay," he seemed taken aback by my tone, "I have. You believe everything because it is the truth. You go back and go over everything."

"I just feel that the best thing for you to do is give—"

"Well, I'm gone," he said with finality. "You're just stalling."

"—yourself up now," I finished.

"Well, Dawn, God bless us all." Click.

If my anger had scared him into hanging up, I didn't care. They had coached me on how to handle him, but I couldn't do it any longer. Anyway, hadn't I kept him on long enough? He had called around 2:20; it was way past 2:30 and they still hadn't caught him? I wanted to scream!

I would not be a victim any longer. I was glad that he knew

I was angry. It was about time the tables were turned and he started fearing me a little bit. The profile that was drawn up showed that he was afraid of dominant women and that he probably had an overbearing mother and a weak father.

But would he call again? As much as I hated it, the truth was that he was still in control. He was the only one who could call. I didn't have a name or a number. I hated the whole situation. He was dangling me and my family like puppets on a string. Once again, it was time to wait.

Friends and family began to show up at our front door to offer condolences, most of whom had been at the funeral. Some of my friends from Carowinds came, and I was deeply touched that they had taken the day off from work. How I wanted to be back there with them again, but it was too much to hope for at this point. Cindy had packed the rest of my clothes and brought them to me. The visit was brief, partly I guessed because it was uncomfortable for them and partly because they had their own lives to get back to. As I watched them drive away, I wanted to run after them and yell, "Take me with you. Please, take me away from this nightmare!"

12

TIME WAS DRAGGING ON. MY LIFE WAS WASTING AWAY. THE HOURS had turned into days and the days into weeks. Would the weeks soon be months, and the months eventually years? There was nothing I could do but wait and pray. I had to believe that God was in control, but I was so weary of the prison my situation had become.

It had been two weeks, and the phone had not rung once. Where was he? The last call had been made from a phone booth in Augusta, Georgia. Had he left the state or even the country? Would we ever hear from him again, or would we all have to live in fear for the rest of our lives?

We didn't have much to do except read newspapers, watch the news on TV, and sit around helplessly. "METTS THINKS ABDUCTOR WAS AT GIRL'S FUNERAL," "REWARD FOR KILLER RAISED," "METTS FEARS KILLER MAY STRIKE AGAIN," "LIVING IN FEAR"—ran the headlines in *The State*. Nothing but dreadful news. That was all the world seemed to offer. How I longed for something to happen . . . something good, if that was possible.

The search, "the most intensive manhunt in the history of the state," as Captain Bob Ford called it, continued fruitlessly. Practically everyone at the funeral had been interviewed, and

Mom, Dad, Robert, and I had spent literally dozens of hours in our den looking at the video of the funeral service, naming everyone we saw and pointing out anyone suspicious. It seemed utterly hopeless. Just as Shari had disappeared, now her killer had. Although our phone had been silent, the sheriff's department had to install six additional telephones to receive the hundreds of calls coming in every day with information for the investigation. A force of 125 men from both the Lexington County and Saluda County Sheriff's Departments continued to work on the case around the clock, as well as SLED, the South Carolina Highway Patrol, the State Department of Wildlife and Marine Resources, and the FBI. But I had to wonder how much longer before they would just call it quits.

A Crimestoppers reenactment of the abduction had been filmed and aired. As a result, a woman who had driven past our house seconds before Shari had disappeared gave a description to authorities of a man who appeared to be trying to talk to Shari as she approached the mailbox. A composite drawing of him appeared in the newspaper practically every day. He looked about thirty-five to forty years old, but resembled no one I knew. Also appearing on the Channel 10 news was the picture of a nine-year-old girl, Debra May Helmick, who had been abducted from the front yard of her Richland County home on Friday, June 14, two weeks after Shari's abduction, and just twenty-four miles from our house. Her father had been inside, barely twenty feet away. As I watched the news each evening, a fear gnawed within me that Shari's killer was at work again. Somehow, I knew it was him. I prayed for her family and for her safety. She was so young— too young to end up the way Shari had.

Because it was still too dangerous to leave our home, we tried to find ways to fill the endless days. One night, Julie, Robert, and I went swimming with all the lights out. The water felt refreshing, the exercise did us good, and it was nice to do something at least halfway normal, but it was scary being in our own back yard in complete darkness. Over the last few weeks, SLED agent Rick McCloud had gotten us some movies, and we'd eaten so many Dominoes pizzas that I found it more difficult with each passing day to button my shorts. Robert and I spent countless hours trying not to laugh out loud at the comedies Rick had rented, for fear that our laughter would have seemed inappropriate and upsetting to Mom or Dad. At least in those few hours, we could escape the horror of what had happened and lose ourselves in another, less painful world.

On many days Rick was our only company, and we grew to love him. His sense of humor never failed, and we soon realized he was a friend who really cared. On one occasion he even took Robert, Julie, and myself to the lake to go skiing on his boat with his family. That was a treat. Of course we were protected by him and another agent, Paul, who also lived at the lake.

Like all my other hamsters, Peachy, Jr., eventually got sick and died. He had been a companion for me on those long, lonely days, and I was sad. Not too long after that, when Ed Smith, the other SLED agent, came for his shift, he handed me a box. Surprised, I opened it and found, to my delight, a cute, furry hamster. I was overwhelmed by his compassion. These men went so far beyond the call of duty and showed again and again that they truly cared for us. I named my new pet Mr. Ed.

Ed got a kick out of that although he tried to hide it. But I saw his beaming smile.

The men of the Lexington County Sheriff's Department and SLED were doing everything in their power to catch the man who'd murdered Shari, and I prayed for them each day. No one believed the suspect had actually carried out his threat to commit suicide.

It was after midnight, June 22, 1985, and I once again couldn't sleep. My sister had been dead for twenty-two days, and it had been two weeks to the day since her murderer had called.

As I lay there, suddenly the phone rang. "Hello," I answered, unprepared now that it had actually happened.

"This is from Shari Faye Smith," the operator said.

Just as I had suspected, he was alive and well. "Yes, I'll take the call."

"Thank you. Is this Dawn?" the operator asked.

"Uh-uh," I answered.

"Thank you," came his voice. How quickly I recognized it. I would never forget it. "Dawn?"

"Yes."

"You know this isn't a hoax, correct?" He sounded strange.

"Right," I responded.

"All right. Did you find Shari Faye's ring?" he asked.

"No, I didn't."

"Okay. I don't know where it is," he said, sounding different from any other time I'd heard him. "You know, uh, God wants you to join Shari Faye. It's just a matter of time. This month, next month, this year, next year. You can't be protected all the time, and you know, uh, have you heard about Debra May Helmick?"

"Uh, no." Terror surged through me. It didn't even register with me that he was talking about the little girl who had been kidnapped eight days earlier.

"The ten-year-old? H-e-l-m-i-c-k?" he reminded me.

"Uh." I finally found my memory. "Richland County?"

"Yeah." He seemed pleased.

"Uh-uh." I was still not over the shock of his sudden threat against me. Where had his sorrow and remorse gone?

"Okay, listen carefully. Go one north—well, one west, turn left at Peach Festival Road or Bill's Grill." He was reading directions again, and I knew all too well what that meant. "Go three and a half miles through Gilbert, turn right, last dirt road before you come to stop sign at Two Notch Road. Go through chain and 'No Trespassing' sign; go fifty yards and to the left; go ten yards. Debra May is waiting. God forgive us all."

John Douglas of the FBI was slipping me a note. "Hey, listen," I said in an effort to keep him from hanging up.

"What?" he asked.

"Uh, just out of curiosity, how old are you?" I asked the only question I could see on the piece of paper.

"Dawn E., your time is near," he said in an evil voice. "God forgive us and protect us all—"

"Wait a second—"

"Good night for now, Dawn—"

"—here," I finished. "What happened to the pictures that you said you were going to send to me? What happened to those pictures that you were going to send?" Terror filled my voice as I struggled to get a conversation going. It had been so long since he had called, and I didn't want to lose him. This might be our last chance to get him, and I felt the weight of that burden like never before. If those directions did lead to the body of that nine-year-old child, he had to be stopped from killing anyone else.

"Apparently the FBI must have them," he answered agitatedly.

"No, sir, because when they have something, we get it too, you know. Are you going to send them?"

"Oh, yes." He seemed far away in his thoughts again.

"I think you're jerking me around because you said they were coming, and they're not here."

"Dawn E. Smith, I must go," he said.

"Listen," I groped, "you said you were going to wait for God's direction—"

"Good night, Dawn, for now."

"You did not give me those pictures," I angrily demanded. I was losing control.

"I'll call you later."

Sheriff Metts, Captain Gasque, and other officers were out the door as soon as we had replayed the tape of the conversation and they had checked the directions I had scribbled down. I knew what this would mean—another body. But why had he called me with the directions instead of the Helmick family? As we waited for news in the early hours of that somber morning, I prayed that somehow this wouldn't be little Debra. *Dear God, she was only nine years old!* My heart ached for her parents. How well we knew what they were going through at that moment.

In the little community of Gilbert, officers found a body right where the caller had said it would be. Like Shari's, the body was badly decomposed from being left out in the June heat for several days and would have to be identified scientifically. It belonged to a young, white female, but nothing else could be determined without a full autopsy. I didn't need a full report to know who that was and who was responsible. Both victims were clad in shorts and had blonde hair and blue eyes; both were kidnapped on Friday afternoons at approximately the same time of day, from in front of their homes, and most importantly, I'd received phone calls with the exact directions to their bodies. We found out that he had called us about the little girl's body only because her family did not have a phone. Debra May Helmick had been kidnapped while playing with her baby brother in the front yard of her family's mobile home.

A neighbor told authorities that she had seen a man, around twenty-eight to thirty-five years old, of medium height and build, with a receding hairline and a beard, pull up to the girl's home in a Monte Carlo. That was the same make of car that had been seen pulling up to our mailbox. The neighbor saw the girl being dragged, kicking and screaming, into the car. I knew in my heart that it was him. Would he strike again? He had said that I was going to be next, and I knew better than ever that he was capable of carrying out his threat. Fear consumed me. Why had the authorities not been able to catch him in three weeks, and how much longer could this go on?

During the time I had been talking to this person in previous calls, believing when he said that he was sorry and wanted to give himself up, he had taken a helpless child and killed her. Now he was ready to make me his third victim. I was outraged. For three weeks this charade had gone on! I could no longer play the game. Next time I would let him have it! I could not tell him again that God could forgive him for what he'd done, for he was not sorry. *Oh, God,* I prayed, *help the officers find him . . . tonight!*

13

JUNE 25TH WOULD HAVE BEEN A DAY OF CELEBRATION—SHARI'S eighteenth birthday. At the suggestion of the FBI, Mom, Dad, Robert, and I would go to the grave site accompanied by deputies and press. We hoped to draw out the suspect and prompt him to call again, since he seemed so interested in anniversaries.

Shari and I both had collected stuffed koala bears, the mascot for Columbia College. I was to take a small koala and put it on the pink flower arrangement on Shari's grave. It seemed a mockery to be doing a manipulative trick, but I wanted this man caught. This was the first time we'd been able to return to the grave since her burial, and I couldn't keep the tears from streaming down my cheeks as I put the koala in place. In my heart, it was a sincere gesture of love for my sister, and it was my way of helping to bring her killer to justice. Mom, Dad, Robert, and I all joined hands around the grave and brokenly prayed, while the clicks of the cameras sounded like firecrackers in the midst of our silence.

Five days had passed since the body of Debra May Helmick had been found, and the killer hadn't kept his promise to call again. I wasn't too surprised; he was such a liar. I wondered if he would ever call again. He was an animal, an

125

animal that needed to be caged. Was he busy plotting how to get me next? I wanted the phone to ring. I wanted something to happen to bring this incredible nightmare to an end.

Finally, when we'd just about given up hope, good news came. Shari's letter had been an answer to my prayers in that it confirmed that Shari knew she was going to be with Jesus and that she was not afraid. Her letter assured me that God had somehow taken away her fear during the whole kidnapping ordeal. But an even greater miracle happened through that last will and testament. Through a series of complex and detailed tests, using a sophisticated apparatus that "reads" molecular changes invisible to the human eye, an FBI document examiner detected impressions left on the legal pad Shari had used to write her letter. Evidently the page that had been used and torn off before her page had had a grocery list and a phone number on it. These had left a slight indention, invisible to the naked eye, in the paper her letter was written on. Finally, after calling all the possible phone numbers, since one of the digits was missing, Southern Bell traced the number to a Huntsville, Alabama, apartment. It was all coming together, and Shari, unknowingly, had helped.

An older married couple living near Lake Murray had gone to Huntsville, Alabama, on vacation and asked an electrician who worked with the husband part time to house-sit for them. The number found on the pad was the place in Huntsville where the couple could be reached in case of an emergency. Their home was only fifteen miles from ours. Soon after deputies had questioned them, it was clear that this married couple in their fifties bore no resemblance to the FBI profile. They had been away on vacation for six weeks.

As they began to tell authorities about their house-sitter,

the truth unfolded. The man was in his mid-thirties, an electrician's helper, divorced, and living with his parents. His twelve-year-old son lived with his ex-wife in another state. He was a meticulous worker who had to have every task explained while he took notes. The couple had noticed that he'd saved newspaper clippings about Shari and had talked obsessively about the murder. He must have lost about ten pounds and seemed somewhat disheveled when they returned home ten days after Debra Helmick's abduction. They had shown him where they kept a loaded .38 pistol, and it was missing. It was found, jammed and dirty, under the mattress of the bed in the room he'd stayed in. Beside it was a *Hustler* magazine with a blonde in bonds on the cover. When the older man heard a recording of the phone calls, he said, "That's Larry Gene Bell. No doubt about it."

At 7:30 A.M. police took Bell into custody at a roadblock as he came off Shull Island on his way to work. He matched the composite drawing to a T—medium build, receding hairline, beard, thirty-six years old.

Dad and Robert had gone out of the house when the sheriff's department called with the news. I could hardly believe that the man who had put our family through all this pain was finally apprehended. The sheriff wanted Mom and me to come down to the department to see if we could make a positive I.D. on the man's voice. I dreaded meeting my sister's murderer face to face, but I wanted to make sure this man would never be free again. As Mom and I rode silently in the back of the patrol car, I knew she was just as apprehensive as I was. I reached over to take her hand in mine, and she smiled weakly at me.

Sheriff Metts told us a few things to expect before the confrontation and explained that the man had not admitted to anything. Then we were escorted into the room where they were holding him. As I came before the man responsible for the horrible things that had happened in the last twenty-eight days of my life, I feared hearing that awful voice in person. The three of us sat there staring at each other. Then he broke the silence by saying something about how sorry he was for our family, but that the Larry Gene Bell sitting in that chair could not have done what had been done to Shari. His sobbing infuriated me as the realization hit. He was, without a doubt, the man who had so vindictively taunted me and my family for an entire month.

"I know that you are the man that killed my sister. I recognize your voice without a doubt," I said, looking him square in the eyes, not flinching. He continued to sob, receiving no pity from me.

Then my mother's voice broke in, and I could hardly believe what I was hearing. "I know that you are the man that killed my daughter, and yet I can honestly look at you and say that I don't even hate you."

He continued to wipe the tears from his face, shocked, as we all were, by her words. It had to be God speaking through her. I sat in awe. His groaning and rambling continued—he couldn't possibly have done it, but the other Larry Bell might have been able to. I was sure it was him. I wanted desperately to wipe the sight of that man sitting across from us in jeans and shirt from my memory forever, but I knew I would never be able to forget either the voice or the face, no matter how hard I tried.

As we pulled back into the driveway of our *own* prison, I couldn't imagine that it was actually over. He had been caught, and I could get on with my life. Yet I realized that it was still a long way from being finished. Truthfully, it would never be over. It would haunt us for the rest of our lives.

The suspect did not confess. After the authorities had futilely interrogated Bell, John Douglas gave it a try. Having interviewed hundreds of psychopaths, Douglas was no stranger to face-to-face confrontations. He offered Bell a face-saving scenario: "There are compulsions in your body and mind that you may not be aware of. People can have blackouts and dark sides to their personalities." Then Douglas directly asked, "When did you first start feeling bad about the crime, Larry?"

"When I saw a photograph and read a newspaper article about the family praying in the cemetery on Shari's birthday," he answered.

"How do you feel about it now?" Douglas asked.

Tears welling, Bell responded, "The Larry Gene Bell sitting here could not have done such a thing. But there's a bad Larry Gene Bell that could have." That was as close as he would ever come to confessing.

Larry Gene Bell had been charged with the kidnapping of Shari Smith, but jurisdictional problems held up his arrest for the murder. Shari had been abducted in Lexington County, but her body was found in Saluda County. The place of the murder was unknown. Of course Bell's neighbors and family described him as kind and gentle and innocent, even though he'd been convicted of at least three violent crimes.

He was first convicted in May 1975 of assault and battery with a knife in Rock Hill, SC. Bell had been sentenced to serve five years in prison, but he was suspended with five years probation and a $1,000 fine. He'd paid the fine; however, he was unable to stay out of trouble while on probation. Just a few months later, he was arrested in Columbia for assaulting a woman. According to the report, he had tried to force the woman into his car after helping her up from a fall. He then had checked himself into a hospital in Columbia, where he was treated for a personality disorder of a "psycho-sexual" nature. He had worked briefly as an airline ticket salesman at Columbia Metropolitan Airport, and then he transferred to Charlotte where he was accused of yet another assault. Back in Columbia, only thirteen months after his first conviction and not long after the Charlotte incident, Bell stood before Circuit Judge Owens T. Cobb in Richland County, who sentenced him to five years in prison for assault and battery, this time involving unlawful possession of a pistol. Cobb urged Bell to obtain psychiatric help in prison and to continue it when he obtained his release on parole. Bell served two years at Central Correctional Institute before parole was granted March 6, 1978. On October 3, 1979, Bell was convicted of making harassing, obscene telephone calls, more than eighty in number, terrorizing a ten-year-old and her mother in Mecklenberg County, NC. He was given a two-year suspended sentence and, once again, placed on five years' probation.

This news infuriated me. If the legal system had taken care of him when he'd first become dangerous, my sister would be alive today! Now I understood what it felt like to be victimized not only by criminals, but by our legal system. Bell was being held while leads and alibis were checked to determine if he was, in fact, the murderer. I prayed that this would be the end to Larry Gene Bell's criminal record. Until he was stopped for good, no driveway, no front yard, no public park, no movie theater, no playground, no pool or pond, no place where children play could be safe . . . ever.

As I looked at the photographs of Shari and Debra that continually appeared in the newspapers, there was something haunting about them—taken when they were both alive and smiling, happy, loved, and safe. They could have been anybody's children, but one of them was my sister. What kind of man could just snuff them into nothingness? I knew all too well. The impression his hard face and squinty, evil eyes had made in my mind could never be erased.

I had to get out of there. I began to ask everyone I could when they thought I would be allowed to go back to Carowinds. It wasn't that I really wanted to go back, but I just couldn't stand one more day in that house. Too many horrors had to be faced—memories on each wall, around each corner, and in each room. My family was shattered, and I couldn't bear just sitting there watching them anymore. The day after the arrest, I left for Charlotte.

All eyes were on me as I reentered the green room of the Chevrolet Theatre where "Celebration" was playing as usual. My friends and troupe members awkwardly welcomed me back, not knowing what to say. I wanted to run back to my car and hide forever. But where could I hide?

As I stepped out onto the lighted stage in my costume and make-up at the opening music, the hot tears on my face took me by surprise. I forced a smile and danced the familiar steps and sang the familiar songs I hadn't done in over a month. I felt so out of place there where I'd felt so happy only a month earlier. God would have to give me the strength to go on, and hadn't He promised that? "Through Christ who strengthens me." I would make it. I had no choice.

The summer heat began to let up slightly, and the afternoon shadows lengthened with the approach of fall. As I packed my things to head back to Columbia College for my senior year, I thought of the excitement Shari and I had shared over her plans to come as a freshman and spend the year together with me. Now that excitement seemed like a distant dream, as if in another life.

I walked across the familiar campus that had been my home for the past three years, and it felt oddly different. I felt different, too. I felt so much older than I had been only three months earlier when I'd left for my summer job. I'd still be performing at Carowinds on the weekends through October, while working on my senior voice recital and preparing for graduation. I felt overwhelmed—not just by school, but also by the pending trial at which I'd have to testify. I did not yet feel that I had reached a beginning.

Trial dates continued to be changed, and it was all over the papers. I found it more than difficult to keep my mind on my studies. Students stared at Julie and me as we made our way about the campus. It was all so painful. How could I have expected life to get back to normal? More than once, I wanted to give up. But something inside kept me going. I knew it was the same something, or Someone, who had kept me talking on those incredibly long and painful phone calls with a murderer. I knew I could have never done that in my own strength and still hold onto my sanity. I had to trust Him to take me on.

Julie continued to be my companion through my countless tearful outbursts, days when I was so full of self-pity that I couldn't see past my pain. She became more to me than just an incredible friend. I felt a kinship with her after all she'd been through with me. She was a sister to me. I saw the love of Jesus being poured out in her beautiful life of obedience and faith, and I depended on her for my own life during that long year. God used her to hold me up when I could hardly walk through the bitter days of grief, and I knew I could never thank her or Him enough.

My life had been so colored by fear that I found it impossible to meet the eyes of a stranger without looking for murder in his eyes. I would never be as friendly, naive, or trusting again. My family had been spun on a hideous emotional yo-yo throughout the previous days of tragedy, rising in hope, and ultimately falling in despair. The grisly shadow of that June tragedy ever loomed over my shoulder with each step forward I tried to take.

14

LARRY GENE BELL WAS BEING HELD AT CCI, COLUMBIA'S HIGH
security facility, while authorities worked on the case. The
newspaper articles continued to say that he claimed he was
innocent. Authorities tried to sort out jurisdictional problems.
Both bodies had been discovered in a different county than the
one in which they were kidnapped. The FBI continued to
review the telephone calls, but these would not be allowed as
evidence in a court of law. They could only be used to help
police identify a suspect. To the officials, the caller's words
presented a picture of a man who appeared compassionate
and religious one minute and brutally insensitive the next.
People who knew Bell identified his voice as the one on the
tapes. There was still no doubt in my mind. Yet the only charge
that had been made was kidnapping. No definite cause of
death could be determined for either victim, and I began to
fear Bell would never be charged with the horrible crimes he
had committed.

School continued to be stressful, for the story stayed in the
news. I resented my professors for expecting me to take tests
and keep my three-year place on the dean's list. I simply
couldn't concentrate on my studies. I would find myself just
sitting, immobile, staring into nothingness. The pressure was

more than I could handle on many days, and I wanted to quit again. I just needed a break . . . from school, from the pending trial, from my pain, from life.

Larry Gene Bell requested to remain in CCI until the trial. Other inmates there called him names such as "baby-killer." A guard had to be stationed outside his cell for his "safekeeping." He feared for his life, and I had to admit that I was glad that he finally could experience the horror he had put his victims through. If he were let into the general prison population, he would not last more than a few minutes.

The months crawled by. Finally a murder warrant came on July 23. On August 12, a Saluda County grand jury indicted Bell for Shari's kidnapping and murder, clearing the way for a trial in that county. His defense attorney asked that the trial be moved some place where potential jurors hadn't been bombarded with press coverage. On September 4, a Lexington County grand jury charged Bell with kidnapping and killing Debra May Helmick. The death penalty would be sought in both cases. Jury selection began on November 4; a pool of 175 was drawn—three times the usual pool for criminal court. Officials knew it would be difficult to find an impartial jury. The trial was scheduled to begin November 11 after Circuit Judge John Hamilton Smith ruled that Bell was mentally competent to stand trial. On November 11, his attorney asked again for a change of venue, but the judge refused, saying he'd try to draw a Saluda County jury first.

But on the opening day of the trial, only one juror had been chosen. The process was painstakingly slow; it seemed that everyone knew about the case. There had been so much press coverage; how could it have been any other way? Five more jurors were seated on November 12, while Bell's attorney continued to plead for the trial to be moved. Because of an article that appeared on the front page of the Saluda weekly newspaper about the trial, the judge agreed with Bell's attorney that most of the people believed Bell was guilty and wanted him hanged. On November 18, Judge Smith announced that he'd try the case in Berkeley County at Moncks Corner, SC, "out of the range of Columbia television stations."

Two months of waiting followed, as both sides finalized their cases. We had to meet with the solicitor to talk about every last detail of our part in the trial. He wanted all four of us there, dressed a certain way, to be seen by the jury every single day. How I dreaded that. In the midst of it all, the first Christmas without Shari was dreadful. Mom and Dad didn't even want to celebrate, but we did, mostly out of a feeling of obligation. As we opened the gifts on Christmas Eve, the usual laughter was replaced with tears of grief. Each of us felt a hollowness as we sat together around the tree. Although the Reason for the season was still with us, we all wanted it to hurry and pass by. Nonetheless, we'd survived the first of many difficult holidays to come.

The court date was set for February 10, 1986. Fear filled my heart as we made our way into the Berkeley County courtroom. I'd never even been inside a courtroom until that day, and I dreaded what was about to take place. I knew we'd have to go back over everything, each painful detail, in order to bring about justice. Although Bell's face had appeared in the papers for the past seven months, my heart still jumped as I watched him enter the courtroom. He looked just as I'd remembered him. He was dressed in a cheap-looking white suit and tennis shoes, looking quite ridiculous, with his hands cuffed. His face held that same smirk I'd seen in so many of the pictures in the newspapers and on the newscasts. His beard was neatly cut, and it looked as if prison life had been treating him well. He had put on a few pounds.

Suddenly he shouted in the crowded room that he was innocent and wouldn't get a fair trial. The outburst took all of us by surprise, as did the round piece of paper clipped to his shirt that said in crude handwriting, probably his: "I'm the victim. Larry Gene Bell. I am innocent." He sickened me.

The next two days were taken up with jury selection, but finally the trial began. When we reentered the dreaded courtroom on that cool Wednesday afternoon of February 12, we didn't know what was ahead or how long it would last. I prayed for God's peace in the midst of the storm.

Testimony began at 3:00 P.M. The prosecution's first witness identified Bell as the driver of a car that had stopped outside our home about the same time Shari had been abducted. "He's sitting right there with a white shirt on," said Terry Butler, a homemaker with two children who lived not far from us.

Another witness, John Ballington, a Lexington County businessman, said that he had seen a car stop near our home at the time Shari had disappeared. Both witnesses said that they had seen Shari approaching the mailbox, the swerving car pull off the pavement, and the brake lights go on. No one had actually seen the abduction.

Thursday, February 13, was an emotional strain. My mother had to take the stand. "I heard Larry Gene Bell talk; then I had a face for that voice I kept hearing over and over and over again," Mom said through a tear-choked voice. To our relief, the tapes of the phone calls, after much argument between both sides, had been allowed as evidence. The jury spent most of that day listening to them. I watched for their reactions as they winced at the cruel things Bell had said, their irritation with him quite obvious. Dad escorted Mom and me into the waiting room. It was too much for Mom to have to go through it all again. We sat in silence with the other witnesses, drinking soft drinks and coffee.

The next day it was my turn to testify, and I prayed I would do a good job. I did not even look at Bell until I absolutely had to, all the while feeling his cold, evil eyes staring at me. Once again, portions of some of the telephone calls were played, to the rapt attention of everyone in the courtroom. I pointed out Larry Gene Bell as the man with whom I had spoken on seven different occasions. When the solicitor asked me if I was absolutely sure, I reiterated that I had no doubt. I did not cry, probably because I was too afraid. All eyes were on me, and I had to do my part.

At times the evidence presented was so grotesque and disturbing that Mom, Robert, and I left and sat in the waiting room. There were plastic bags with all sorts of things in them—a few strands of Shari's blonde hair, pieces of jewelry she'd been wearing at the time of her death (including her high school ring), the clothes she'd been wearing at the time of her disappearance, her bandana that we believed she'd thrown out the window of her kidnapper's car to help lead us to her, the letter she'd written to us—the list went on and on. Pornographic magazines showing women in bonds had been found in Bell's room at his parents' home. When they were about to bring in the mattress from the bed where Shari had been tied, Dad quickly escorted us out again. We sat through eight long days of witnesses and waiting, and then the prosecution rested.

During that time in the periods spent in the waiting room, I had to make myself study. Robert's teachers had been very understanding, and he was able to do much of his schoolwork there as well. Although my personal world seemed to be on hold because of the trial, the rest of the world continued as usual, and I had to try to keep up. There were exams, pieces of music to be orchestrated, and then there were my English, Italian, French, and German songs and arias that had to be memorized for my senior recital, without which I would not graduate. The pressure mounted with every day, and I felt I'd never be fully prepared for my recital. I refused to think of putting it off until the next year. I had to graduate with Julie and the rest of my class. Rick would pick me up very early in the morning on many days to speedily get me back to Moncks Corner after taking me to the campus for tests or rehearsals. My energy was running out.

On Monday, February 17, Lt. Larry Walker of the Charlotte Police Department testified that during an interview at the Central Correctional Institution in Columbia the previous July 14, Bell had told investigators about Shari's slaying. Walker went on to say that Bell had told him, "The hands of Shari Faye Smith were crossed as if in praying when she died," and that he'd held her head and given her a drink of water. The hushed courtroom listened intently as Walker said that Bell had asked Shari if there was anything she wanted before she "departed." Bell had also told Walker that "when Shari Smith died, her eyes were closed, not like in the movies when people die with their eyes open." Bell also told him that after the crime, he "came back home and cleaned everything up and put it in a green dumpster," and then took "a good, strong shower."

That repulsed me. I prayed the jury would remember and

believe what the lieutenant had said, since it was obvious Bell was not going to cooperate. It was the closest thing we had to a confession, and I was grateful for it.

Disagreements continued throughout the trial concerning Bell's mental state. Two doctors who had testified for the defense said that Bell was psychotic, but under cross-examination, our doctor said the condition would not be considered insanity in the legal sense of the word. I breathed another prayer of gratitude and hoped there would be no more outbursts from him that might alter that decision. I knew that the man I'd talked with on the phone over seven months earlier was most definitely sick, but he wasn't crazy. He had known very well what he was doing. We were all tiring of him, including the judge and jury.

Later that day, the defense opened its case, and Bell testified. Asked how old he was, Bell replied, "Silence is golden." Then, after a pause, he said, "I'm thirty-seven." He then asked to meet with his attorney, and court was recessed while the two huddled for about twenty-five minutes. I knew this would not be over anytime soon. Judge Smith then adjourned court for the day.

Next day, Bell once again took the stand, after many members of his family and friends had testified about what a kind, calm, caring man he was and that he was incapable of such crimes. "This is very bizarre and unusual, like all other things in my life," he began. "I had a vision of Shari Smith, and I shall not explain it because the family is present." I knew all too well the game he was trying to play with the jury, and I wasn't buying it.

I shuddered as he looked our way. His eyes rested on me as I kept my gaze downward. He mentioned also having visions of Debra May Helmick and her kidnapping. While his attorney asked Bell what the dreams were about, he only responded, "Silence is golden." He said that he was taking his mother home from a doctor's appointment at the time Shari was abducted. She agreed to this in her testimony as well. Obviously, she was lying! He also said that prosecution witnesses who identified his voice as the one on the tapes were "poisoned by pretrial publicity. A blind man could see it, and a deaf man could hear it."

Bell talked about his childhood and defended his sanity. He said that he had seen visions of God. He stood at the witness stand with a red Bible and a book by Rev. Billy Graham in front of him, motioning as he spoke, like some sort of preacher or evangelist. He said that he preferred to stand while on the witness stand because "unfortunately there are no chairs at the gates of Hell. Either you sit on the floor or on a hard bed."

He crazily continued, "Things come in any category from God through the Lord Jesus to the person. I don't have a mental problem, although they think I do."

Six hours of this tiresome rambling went by, with Judge Smith asking him many times to sit down, calm down, or leave the courtroom.

"Mr. Bell, I'm out of patience. Please sit in the witness box," Judge Smith ordered.

"The witness is supposed to stand out here—that's what they did in eighteenth-century England," Bell mocked, chuckling.

"You're out of time and out of place," the judge wearily said. "Sit where you're supposed to, or you'll be removed, and the trial will go on without you."

"Okay, okay." Bell complied. "You'd really have my own trial without me? Can I ask a question, Your Honor?"

"What is it?"

"I'm asking Dawn Smith to marry Larry Gene Bell," he stated, looking directly at me, as if he expected a response. I thought I must have heard wrong.

As Solicitor Myers continued his cross-examination on the next day, February 19, Bell would only answer his questions with his usual response, "Silence is golden." He continued his defiant exchanges with the solicitor and refused to answer questions about the abduction or the "visions" he'd claimed to have had of Shari's death.

"Apparently you didn't do your homework last night," Bell told Myers. "I said yesterday that silence was golden, my friend. You are crossing a line from business to personal things. Maybe you are deaf."

During the testimony, Myers had to steer Bell back to the line of questioning repeatedly as he rambled or refused to answer. The judge denied a defense motion for mistrial, saying Bell had proved he could understand and answer questions. "If the question presents harm to him, then he starts his supposed wandering," he calmly said. The judge could see right through him and his schemes.

As we sat tensely through the second day of this behavior, Bell complained to the court that Myers was trying to trick him into confessing. "You can't confuse me," he blurted out. "I don't know why you're wasting the court's valuable time. Saluda County is already in the red. I'm not going to confess to something I'm not responsible for. I don't want to tell you anything about it. Give me liberty or give me death."

Myers asked Bell if he recalled telling doctors at the

Veterans Administration Hospital in Columbia in 1975 that he had made up stories about having visions whenever he experienced legal problems.

He responded, "Back then I was confused. I called them nightmares and dreams. Now I call them visions."

Bell could not be executed if the verdict returned was guilty but mentally ill, and he knew it. However, he denied he was disturbed. "I do not have a mental illness. But you could never convince doctors of that. I've talked to them all my life and told them over and over again there's nothing wrong with me. Food for thought. Gifted, dumb or a fruitcake? You pick one. I've been poisoned."

After one too many outbursts, the judge ordered Bell to be taken out of the courtroom. Testimony was stopped for about two and a half hours while he was examined by medical experts, and attorneys argued whether he was able to continue.

During the competency hearing, his attorney asked Bell what he would say if he were instructed not to talk about me. There was a long pause as Bell leafed through the Bible he'd held in his hands over the last several days. Then, without apparent reference, he said, "Food for thought. Like I said earlier on the record, if you believe this is truth, the Mona Lisa is a man and silence is golden, my friend."

He then returned to his seat at the defense table despite his attorney's attempts to ask additional questions. "I'm tired," he wearily said, as if he'd given up. "Let's get this over with."

"Are you going to cooperate with me?" his attorney asked.

"I've turned my life over to you, and it's in your hands," Bell responded before sitting down.

Another clinical psychologist testified that when she had

examined Bell the day before, he had shown psychotic behavior. He had told her that President Reagan would be coming to the trial, that he could have solved the Lebanon hostage crisis, and that if he were sent to the electric chair, he could use special powers to prevent anyone from throwing the switch. He also said that this trial was being held to plug national security leaks. She concluded that he was most probably psychotic at that point, simply out of touch with reality.

Still another doctor took the stand to testify that Bell was unable to proceed, but said he might be able to recover with rest and a sedative to reduce stress. It seemed that everyone was more concerned about Bell and his state of mind than about my family and what he'd put us through! Yet, another psychiatrist said that he thought Bell was "attempting to create confusion" and that he had "a good knowledge of what's going on in court." Judge Smith agreed, saying that Mr. Bell did have a certain flair for the theatrical.

His attorney was trying to show that Bell was mentally ill at the time of the crime and unable to follow the law. That was and is the standard for a possible verdict of guilty but mentally ill. I could not understand how a man could defend someone like Larry Gene Bell. I wondered how his attorney could sleep at night.

As Mr. Myers rose to give his closing statements, I prayed he'd say the right things. During his closing arguments, he called Bell a sadist, a definite threat to women, a sexual deviant. Myers said that Bell should get an Academy Award for acting as though he were mentally ill. He reemphasized to the jurors that the only time Bell had ever sought psychiatric help was when he was in trouble with the law. And, again noting that an "anonymous" caller had taunted our family in the days after the abduction and had detailed the murder, he asked the jury, "Was that out of touch with reality when in reality it is sadistic?"

However the defense attorney urged the jury to return a verdict of guilty but mentally ill. It made me nervous to think that his words were the last the jury would hear before leaving the courtroom to decide upon a verdict. He was definitely good. "It seems to me," he cleverly began, "the state of South Carolina is asking us to bury our heads in the sand and go back to the sixth century when people with mental problems were treated like everybody else." He concluded that Bell was not insane at the time of the crime and knew right from wrong, but said that his mental condition, borderline psychotic, made it impossible for him to conform his actions to the requirements of the law. He stated that this was the legal test for a verdict of guilty but mentally ill.

As his attorney was about to finish his argument, Bell surprised everyone by suddenly interrupting, "Judge Smith, today's the Sabbath. Legally and in the eyes of God, I should take the stand."

The judge told Bell to sit down. He did, but moments later he interrupted the proceedings again. The jury was sent out, and the judge told Bell that if he wasn't quiet, he could not remain in the courtroom. Bell then motioned toward me and said, "In my hand no price I bring, simply to the cross I cling. Legally and in the eyes of the law, I want to ask Miss Dawn Smith to marry me, Mr. Gene Bell." My stomach turned.

After a twenty-minute recess, the jury returned. Almost immediately, Bell stood up and said to the judge, "Mr. Smith, legally and in the eyes of God, I'm tired, I'm cold, and I'm hungry."

Again, the jury was sent out. The judge asked Bell if he would disrupt the proceedings again if he were allowed to remain. "Yes, legally and in the eyes of God—in due respect for both sides," he answered. He was escorted from the courtroom.

Later, when he did return to the courtroom at the judge's permission, he remained quiet. He looked at me a number of times as I sat behind the prosecutor's table, trying to hide myself from his gaze. Robert, during the entire trial, had acted as my shield, blocking Bell's view of me. When Bell would stare at me, Robert would lean forward and look him square in the eyes until Bell had to look away.

Fourteen days had passed since the beginning of the trial, and I was exhausted from having to travel back and forth from Moncks Corner to Columbia, trying to keep up with my school work, opera rehearsals, and rehearsals for my senior recital. I thought I would go crazy, but somehow I made it through. Not somehow, I knew, but Someone helped me. I would not have made it without the steady hand that had guided me and much of the time carried me.

Once again, we were in the waiting room—this time waiting for the verdict. Mom, Dad, Robert, and I didn't have much to say. We could only pray that the jury would find him guilty. The clock on the wall ticked loudly as we sat nervously around the big table in the center of the room. Twenty minutes . . . thirty minutes . . . forty minutes . . . fifty minutes passed with no word. Dad paced the room. Finally, after fifty-five minutes had crept by, the jury reached a decision. We all nervously filed back into the stuffy courtroom. How I hated to have to see him even one more time. I prayed once more for the guilty verdict. There had been five verdicts to be considered: not guilty,

guilty, guilty but mentally ill, not guilty by reason of insanity, or involuntary manslaughter. I didn't doubt he'd be found guilty. Solicitor Donnie Myers had done such an incredible and thorough job in presenting all the evidence for the case. But I feared a verdict of involuntary manslaughter, guilty but mentally ill, or insanity. With any of these, more psychological tests would have to be done, and only God knew when it would ever end.

As the jury made their way back to their seats, I stole a glance to see if I could read their faces. I could tell nothing.

"Have you reached a decision, Mr. Foreman?" Judge Smith asked formally. I jumped at his question. This was it.

"We have, Your Honor," the man replied. He seemed nervous.

Fear gnawed at my stomach. I stared straight ahead at the judge. I heard the word *guilty* once, for the charge of kidnapping, and I breathed a sigh of relief, but that wasn't what I was waiting for. I heard *guilty* again, and I waited to make sure no other words would be attached to it. Larry Gene Bell had been found guilty of both the kidnapping and murder of Shari Faye Smith. Mom, Dad, Robert, and I exchanged hugs, as tears of relief flowed from our eyes. Yet no smiles crossed our faces. This was not a happy time; it was nothing more than a long-awaited moment of justice. The sense of finality I had expected did not come. I knew we still had to go through the sentencing phase. I looked over at the jurors who had had to leave their families behind and take on such an overwhelming task. I saw pity in their eyes as they watched us leave the courtroom. *Thank you,* I wanted to shout to them! No words were ever exchanged between them and us, but I hoped that somehow they'd know how indebted my family and I would always be to them for the sacrifice each had made to bring about justice.

Bell had shown no emotion when the verdict was read. I thought it bitterly funny that he didn't save one more outburst for the grand finale. His play was over. As he left the building, he said to reporters desperate to get a statement, "Silence is golden, my friend." Sunday, February 23, 1986, ended one of the longest trials of my life, not only the trial that had taken place in the courtroom, but the one that had been raging in my heart for the past eight months. My precious sister's murderer had been found guilty and would never have the chance to hurt anyone again. Tuesday the sentencing phase would begin, and the state was seeking the death penalty.

After two more weeks in that dreadful courtroom, Larry Gene Bell, the thirty-seven-year-old electrician and murderer, did receive the death penalty. I knew there would be appeals and more appeals, but a peace in my heart told me I'd never have to fear him again. All along I'd been afraid of the possibility of other sentences and possible parole. Now I could rest at ease. He was out of my life for good, and I was ready to move on.

15

ONLY A FEW MONTHS LATER, MY LIFE TOOK A TURN THAT GREATLY helped the process of moving on. Looking back, I think the new challenge came at exactly the right time. It took my mind off our tragedy and completely caught me up in something exciting and worthwhile.

Our family—the girls, that is—never missed a beauty pageant. We would settle down in front of the TV with popcorn and cokes to watch the Miss South Carolina and Miss America Pageants every year. The year I was close to graduating from high school, we were watching, attention glued to the competition, when Shari had looked over at me and said seriously, "Dawn, you need to enter the pageant now 'cause these girls are getting uglier and uglier every year!"

I could never imagine myself up on that stage, much less on television! We had both competed in local and school contests, but a real pageant? No way! All those girls seemed and looked so perfect, and I was far from that!

My voice teacher, Mrs. Palmer, though, had another idea. She'd had several of her students at Columbia College compete in the Miss South Carolina Pageant over the years, including one who had placed first. Mrs. Palmer told me that the scholarships the girls had won had helped them with their education and careers. I was about to graduate and had not decided what to do afterward. I remembered my commitment to full-time Christian service in high school, but I began to think about what *I* wanted to do with my music—telling myself that I'd still be serving God, whatever I did. I was planning on going back to Carowinds for my third summer and then looking into graduate school to work on my Master's degree in vocal performance. Mr. and Mrs. Palmer continued to encourage me to at least think about entering the pageant, but facing the swimsuit competition made me hesitate. I'd feel ridiculous strolling around on a stage in a swimsuit in front of all those people. But much deeper than that was the feeling that I was not ready to face the public after what I'd been through.

However with the Palmers' and Julie's encouragement, I entered the Miss Columbia Pageant. I didn't own one thing appropriate to wear in it, and Angela Powers, a friend who had been third runner-up to Miss South Carolina a few years earlier, helped me scrounge around and borrow an evening gown, talent gown, and swimsuit. I couldn't believe what I was doing, but I continued to think about the scholarship money that would help me get to Indiana University, one of the best music schools in the country.

Mom, Dad, Robert, and Nana came to the pageant, along with Julie and Cindy, and my boyfriend—my cheering section. In the interview competition, the judges and their questions made me nervous, and I felt as if I had really bombed. As I made my way out onto the stage in my aqua swimsuit, I wanted to run right back off! I prayed the judges and audience couldn't see my legs quivering. Dad just looked down as his little girl came out, took her turns, and quickly left the stage.

His younger sister, Sue, had been Miss South Carolina in 1965, and he was not too thrilled about his daughter participating in the pageant. With all our family had been through and the publicity involved, we were afraid the press would bring everything to the surface again. After much prayer and thought, I decided that, since I didn't have any money and wanted to continue my education and pursue a singing career, I needed to do it. I had to admit I was truly glad that part of the evening was over though.

I sang my talent presentation with everything I had in me, held out the high C at the end of the aria for all it was worth, and actually enjoyed that part of it. Singing was like second nature to me, and I felt sure I would at least win the talent competition. I had chosen to sing "Ah! Je Veux Vivre" from *Romeo and Juliet* by Charles Gounod. The applause raised my confidence, and we finished evening gown competition.

As we stood in a line and waited for the announcement, I glanced to my left and to my right, wondering which contestant might be chosen and praying I'd hear my own name as the winner.

"The talent winner tonight is Dawn Elizabeth Smith," the overweight emcee proclaimed. I was thrilled as I moved forward to receive my trophy.

"The swimsuit winner for tonight is . . ." I knew it definitely wouldn't be me. "Ronetta Hatcher!" I had guessed it would be her. She had won Miss Columbia College the year before, and I had been her first runner-up. She was beautiful, with long dark hair and dark eyes, and was very bright as well. I felt that if she did win Miss Columbia, she deserved it. Somehow I knew that one day she'd even make a great Miss South Carolina, which later she did.

Well, here goes, I thought to myself. "And our new Miss Columbia, who will go on to compete in the Miss South Carolina Pageant this July is . . ." I held my breath as I held my stomach in in my tight gown.

Who? When the name was announced, I had to look to see who it was. Disappointment washed over me. All I had to show for this night of humiliation was a stupid trophy. How many bills was that going to pay? Mrs. Palmer, Julie, and Angela met me with half-hearted smiles, saying that I should have won, and next time I would, etc., etc. As I angrily packed my things into the back of my gold Chevrolet Spectrum, my surprise graduation gift from Mom and Dad, I told Julie I'd never do that again. Evidently I had not been ready, in any way. But she wouldn't take no for an answer. For some reason, Julie always seemed to believe in me even when I didn't believe in myself.

The Miss Liberty Pageant, an open pageant, meaning any girl in the state could enter since the town of Liberty was too small to have a closed pageant, would be in just a few months. Julie, Angela, and Mrs. Palmer tried to coax me into trying again. But I just didn't want to turn into a professional con-testant. I either wanted to win or forget it. They kept telling me that I could be Miss South Carolina. I wanted to know how in the world they expected me to be Miss South Carolina when I couldn't even win Miss Columbia!

I couldn't believe I was doing it again as Julie and I rode to Liberty on April 3. But I'd worked hard on preparing myself for this pageant, and this time I was determined to win. I'd learned the hard way that hodgepodging just wouldn't do it. On faith I had two gowns made, one for evening gown and one for talent. My evening gown was elegant, gold-sequined with rhinestone appliques around the sweetheart neckline. My talent gown was simple. It was all white, with a full skirt, belted waistline, and a ruffle with pearls and flowers all around the neckline, with a matching headpiece. My swimsuit was blue, to match my eyes. I prayed that if the Lord really wanted this for me that He'd help me to do my best. From my meager salary at Carowinds I would be making payments on the competition attire forever unless I could win. The glamour, however, faded quickly as we entered the motel in the nearby town of Easley, SC, and the first thing we saw was a dead cockroach on the bathroom floor!

With the excitement of the rehearsal over, Julie and I sat up late as she told me that she'd scoped all the other girls out and felt that I was going to win. She definitely had the gift of encouragement.

As I walked into the interview session the next morning wearing a simple pink dress, I wasn't too nervous, and I actually enjoyed myself. They were much kinder than the judges had been in Columbia, and they even wished me a happy birthday. It was April 4, 1986, my twenty-second birthday. I hoped I would receive the present I really wanted—the crown!

Mom, Dad, Robert, Nana, Julie, and several other friends were there to support me. Even after almost a year, it seemed so strange not to see Shari's face among them. Oh, how I missed my sister.

After all the competition was completed, we stood once again in a line as the winners were called out. I had watched Sherry Thrift, the reigning Miss South Carolina and first runner-up to Miss America, as she'd emceed the pageant. I admired her for her Christian commitment and friendliness. She'd been so kind and helpful to each contestant, and her example helped me realize that it was actually possible to win and yet remain a real, down-to-earth person. Just before the evening had started, she had gathered us all together, and we held hands in a circle as she led us in prayer. She was a dynamic blonde—blue-eyed, petite, and only five feet tall. Her height gave me some hope, since I was only five feet, two and a half myself. As she called out the talent award, I hoped it would be me.

"Our Elizabeth Hayes talent award tonight goes to . . . Dawn Elizabeth Smith!" The screams from my fan club thrilled me as I accepted my trophy and headed back to my place in line.

As Sherry began the next announcement, I knew I might as well be comfortable right where I was. "Our swimsuit winner tonight is . . . are you ready?" she cutely asked. "Dawn Elizabeth Smith!" I was in shock. There must have been some mistake. How could I have won with my "bird legs," as Robert and Shari had always called them? If I had actually won the swimsuit trophy, could this mean what I hoped?

As Sherry announced the runners-up, I was so glad she didn't call my name, but I was afraid she might not call it out again.

"Ladies and gentlemen, the moment we've waited for tonight, our new Miss Liberty, who will go on to compete for the title of Miss South Carolina this July in Greenville is . . . Dawn Elizabeth Smith!"

I couldn't believe it! I had actually won! I was so excited I didn't know what to do. Tears came to my eyes as the former Miss Liberty, who had become Miss South Carolina and first runner-up to Miss America, pinned the crown on my head. Now I hoped I was on my way to do the same thing. As Mom and I drove back to school, we were both jubilant. This had been a dream that Mom, Shari, and I had shared. Mom had always been supportive, telling me she believed in me. I kept saying over and over, "Mom, can you believe it? I'm going to be in the real Miss South Carolina Pageant in just two months! Oh my gosh! Whether I win or not, I am actually going to be in the Miss South Carolina Pageant!"

After a tearful graduation, I returned to Carowinds and began performing in the upbeat new show "Gotta Dance." It was a great show, and I was enjoying my job, but I hoped I would not be there after the first of July. I knew I needed to move on, win or lose the pageant. God was again working on my heart. Every single day during our breaks between the four to six shows, I'd practice walking in my three-inch heels, and I'd ask the sound man in the theater if he would run my orchestrated tape of "Ah! Je Veux Vivre" so that I could practice. Once home and totally exhausted, I'd read the newspaper and watch the news to keep up with current events for the interview phase of competition. I had decided that since I was going to do this, I would do it right.

The Miss Liberty Pageant committee encouraged me with notes and messages saying that I would not only be the next Miss South Carolina, but also the next Miss America! That was another matter . . . I just needed to do one thing at a time. My sponsor for the week of competition was the Liberty Businessmen's Association, and they had not forgotten anything. As I checked into the Hyatt in Greenville the night before rehearsals, I felt really blessed to have such a great group of supporters. I hoped and prayed I would make them proud and glad to have worked with me. The pressure was great since Sherry Thrift had been Miss South Carolina and had come so close to being Miss America. I wanted to follow in her footsteps, which were pretty big for a size four.

The other contestants were so beautiful, just as I had suspected. Even though we were to spend practically every waking minute in the Greenville Memorial Auditorium for rehearsals all that week, up on our feet learning choreography and staging, we all wore our best clothes and high heels. It was ridiculous, but we all wanted to look our best. The exciting week brought little sleep and lots of stress. I felt very good about my seven-minute private interview with the judges. They had all been gracious and kind as they asked their questions, some of these very difficult. Each contestant had to write an autobiographical sketch, and I had written in mine about being in church all of my life, accepting Christ at the age of nine, my education and hopes for the future, about how God's grace had brought me through the tragic loss of my sister, and how I was ready to be Miss South Carolina. Shirley Cothran, a former Miss America and judge who was also a Christian communicator, asked me the strangest question. As she looked over my sketch, she simply said, "Dawn, do you think you would be able to handle the stress that would go along with being Miss South Carolina well?"

I knew exactly what she meant, and I answered, "Yes, I definitely could . . . definitely." I said no more, but as our eyes met, I somehow knew that she understood what I'd been through and didn't need any more explanation.

My group had evening gown on the first night of competition. It was, to me, the simplest one. We had to walk out on stage, say a short speech that we'd prepared, do our turns in front of the judges, and that was it.

"With a degree in vocal performance from Columbia

College, I plan to continue my studies at Indiana University to obtain a Master's degree in voice and pursue a career in the performing arts. I am contestant number 13, Dawn Elizabeth Smith, Miss Liberty." I made it through without stumbling over my words or my feet. Although no winner was announced for evening gown, I felt I did pretty well. My dress had looked lovely as it shimmered under the lights.

The next night was my night—talent competition! I was excited all that day as I practiced in the hallways of the auditorium on our breaks. I'd practiced long and hard for the past two months, strengthening my performance, and I prayed I'd do my best. As I took my bow at the end of my performance, to my surprise, the Miss South Carolina Orchestra stood to their feet!

Finally it was time to announce the winners. I began to tremble. Oh, how I wanted to win. There was so much talent there from all over the state, but still I hoped I had a chance. Sherry was the emcee for the state pageant as well, and I leaned forward, intent on hearing her announcement. "Our preliminary talent competition winner tonight is . . . Dawn Elizabeth Smith, Miss Liberty!"

I was thrilled! As I made my way down the runway, I knew I had to be beaming. I hoped to win the pageant overall, but even if I didn't, I'd won in the phase of competition most important to me.

I was on top of the world, as tired as I was, but I wasn't looking forward to the rest of the night's competition. My group finally had swimsuit. Although I had won it at Miss Liberty, this was entirely different. Some girls on that stage had competed in the state pageant before, and they knew more about what they were doing than I. Some of them had even placed the previous year. Nonetheless, I felt very good about the new suit I'd gotten for the state competition, a white "super suit." As we stood about the stage, all forty-nine of us in our closing gowns, I just hoped I'd done well enough to make it into the top ten to compete on television on the next night.

"Our preliminary swimsuit winner tonight is . . . Dawn Elizabeth Smith, Miss Liberty!"

What? I was almost afraid to step forward for fear I'd heard wrong. No one else was moving, and all their heads were turned toward me. I could not believe that I had just won the swimsuit award in my group at the Miss South Carolina Pageant!

I was a double-preliminary winner, and my picture had been in *The State* newspaper for the past two days. Yet I did not feel overly confident. I had one more night to go. Besides, Debbie Brown, Miss Berea, the beautiful, tall, blonde flautist, was also a double-preliminary winner.

We spent that entire long Saturday in the cold auditorium rehearsing for TV. It was exciting, but I was so tired. My parents, Robert, Nana, Uncle Ricky, and Aunt Beverly, and many of my cousins had been there throughout the week to encourage me, as well as Julie and other friends. They'd sent me notes every day, along with my Liberty friends, and really kept me going. As show time approached, I sat quietly in my dressing room while the other girls excitedly chattered among themselves. I wanted to win so badly, but I kept telling God that I only wanted what He wanted, knowing His plan would be better than my own. I felt I had a real chance, and that both thrilled and frightened me. Could I be named Miss South Carolina in only two short hours?

After the opening number, the top ten finalists were called. The emcee had called eight names, and I was still standing right where I'd been since the close of the production number. *Oh, Lord, surely I've made it.* Finally, I heard my name, the next to the last finalist, and we were off to change into our swimsuits. Then it was time for talent competition, and lastly, evening gown. I gave it everything I had. I was so nervous, but I also felt exhilarated at the excitement permeating the air, cameras and hot lights adding to the magic of that evening.

Sherry Thrift made her final official walk as Miss South Carolina and gave her farewell speech with the music of "To God Be the Glory" in the background. She unashamedly proclaimed her faith in Jesus Christ, and it was evident that she gave Him the glory for all that she'd done. She was truly a winner, not just because of her crown, but because of her sweet, humble spirit and genuine love for people. I prayed that if I should be crowned her successor in the next few minutes, I would be just as bold a witness and continue the wonderful work she'd begun.

The fourth and third runners-up had been named, and now it was time for the second runner-up. My stomach felt as if it had crept up into my throat as she began to read the name. I was so afraid it was going to be me, since I'd finished third in the other pageants. Whew! Miss Berea! "The first runner-up and winner of a . . ." I prayed it would not be me—not yet. ". . . is Miss Sumter, Suzanne Grace West!" She had been a wonderful person to be with that week and a very talented ballerina. I could see on her face the obvious disappointment at coming so close. I wondered if all the time I'd been wishing my name wouldn't be called yet, in fact, it wasn't going to be called at all!

"And now," the emcee began, "the finest that South Carolina has to offer." What was he saying? That didn't make much sense, but I was listening with all my heart. "Your new Miss South Carolina 1986, to compete for the title of Miss America in Atlantic City this September is . . ." The drumroll was unnecessary since I was sure my heart was doing a fine job of that. "Miss Liberty, Dawn Elizabeth Smith!"

I had won! Tears of joy and gratitude streamed from my eyes as I stepped forward and Sherry pinned the much-coveted crown on my head. *Thank you, Lord,* I breathed. I motioned a most sincere thank you to the judges as I made my way down that famous runway on which Miss South Carolinas had walked all those years on TV as Mom, Shari, and I had watched. As I waved to the cheering crowd, I couldn't believe it was actually happening to me! I was Miss South Carolina! How I wished Shari could be there to share this moment with me. The audience was on its feet as I waved to them.

Mom, Dad, and Robert made their way through the crowd up on the stage, and I could see that they'd also been crying. Mom and Dad rushed over to hug me, their pride evident. I knew their tears were mixed with both joy and sorrow, just as mine were. This was Shari's dream for me—something she had believed I could do. I looked over Mom's shoulder to see Robert, over six feet tall now, with red, swollen eyes. As I reached out for him, I knew he was proud of his big sister. It was such a special moment. After so much pain and sadness, it was good to see smiles and tears, not of grief, but of joy. Nana made her way up to us through all of the photographers and press waiting for a statement and said something about not only being the mother of a Miss South Carolina, but now the grandmother of one! Julie was there to join in the celebration, and I could see all over her beautiful face that she was just as thrilled as I was. I felt so blessed in that moment, not just because of the tilting crown on my head, but because of the special gifts of family and friendship there to share it with me.

After pictures and interviews, I was whisked away into a dressing room where I was to meet my hairdresser, Jim Leone. He immediately began to brush out the hair spray that I had drenched my hair with to make sure it held up under the hot lights. He re-rolled and styled my hair. Tom Faircloth, who worked with the pageant, asked me about my speech for the ball.

"Speech?" I asked in astonishment. Nobody had mentioned a speech before now. Would I have to speak to the crowd that had assembled in that huge formal ballroom? Were all those people in there waiting to see if I met their approval as Miss South Carolina? Could I pass? I'd never had to give a speech before. What would I say? Gail Sanders, the wardrobe consultant, began to give me ideas. Rita Allison, who would be my traveling companion in Atlantic City, stood nearby, and the three of us began to quickly list things that I could say and needed to say. I felt better.

As I was escorted into the glamorous ballroom and ushered up to my place at the head table, all in the room were standing to their feet. For me? I looked out over a sea of faces whose eyes were all on me. I wasn't sure I was prepared for this. Many of the pageant officials, including Gail's husband, Joe Sanders, President and Executive Director of the Miss South Carolina Pageant, made speeches. My family sat at the table just in front of me, with big smiles. Sherry Thrift and her family were close beside them. As Sherry made her way up to say a few words at the podium, I knew I was next.

The applause diminished, and Joe made the introduction. My nerves were working full blast, and I silently prayed that God would give me the words to say.

"First of all," I began, "I would like to thank God who has made this all possible." I didn't know what I would say, but I felt assured that He was giving me the words. "Without Him, I would not be here." How true. It was a miracle that I was standing there. "My mother, father, brother, and grandmother are all sitting here, and I'd like to thank them and tell them that I love them . . ." I found it impossible to hold back my emotions.

I knew I'd never be able to sleep that night, as I bade my family good night and Gail and I made our way up to the room where we would stay for the next week.

I had received so many beautiful gifts at the awards ball— an $8,000 scholarship, a silver fox coat, jewelry from the Jewelry Warehouse—official jeweler of the Miss South Carolina Pageant, cosmetics, skin-care products, and the list went on and on. I was truly amazed at what was happening to me. Somehow I knew in that moment that my life would never be the same.

●

"I do not want to be!" I shouted out into the darkness of the room, bolting straight up in the bed. Gail, scared to death, reached for the light and asked me what in the world was wrong. I couldn't remember my dream . . . nightmares had become so frequent in the nights since we'd lost Shari. I'd have

164

the same dream over and over—that Shari had been taken, but that she had escaped and was alive. The dream would wind around a painful trail of pain, questions, horrid answers as to what really happened to her, but at least she was alive. Then I'd wake up, thinking the tragedy had only been a horrible nightmare and that the dream was reality. After I'd wake up thoroughly, the painful truth would hit. Mom, Dad, and Robert all had bad dreams.

It seemed I was plagued by them. Crazed men chasing me, trying to kill me, Shari's horrified face, dreams of what had happened to her . . . they went on and on and on. I'd awake in a pool of sweat. Once I calmed down, we slept the few hours until morning.

I awoke early. Jim Leone came in and did my hair. I put on the white, hand-crocheted dress I'd worn in my interview, since it was the only decent one I owned and got ready for my first press conference. Mom and Dad met me in the conference room, and we hugged. We were still all in shock, and I was nervous, wondering what the questions would be. So this was what it felt like to be Miss South Carolina. I had always wondered. I felt no different really. But everyone was treating me differently. I was Miss South Carolina, but to Mom, Dad, and me, I was still just Dawn.

The reporters arrived, and the questions began. They asked how it felt to be Miss South Carolina and what I planned on doing during my reign. Then my excitement turned into dread as the next question came out. They wanted to know about the "tragedy." I shared as best I could how the Lord had brought us through the loss of Shari, and the story appeared in the paper the next day. "DAWN OF A NEW DAY" was the headline. The story went on to tell about how I, with my faith in God, had sought the Miss South Carolina title after the brutal death of my sister just a year before. It felt strange to see my story and my words quoted in newspapers across the state, but that was only the beginning of countless articles and interviews that would focus on the difficult turn of events in my life. It seemed everyone wanted to know about "the tragedy." I wondered if I was ready to be the public figure I had become overnight. How I hoped it really would be a new day for me and my family.

16

THAT FIRST WEEK OF BEING MISS SOUTH CAROLINA WASN'T AS glamorous as I had expected. I spent it filling out all the detailed paperwork for the Miss America Pageant, daily working out with my new weight coach, Jack Pollard—who I thought would literally kill me—practicing my talent, attending my weekly lesson with Mrs. Palmer, reading the papers, and watching the news. Then there were wardrobe fittings and shopping sprees. I had only seven weeks to prepare for Atlantic City. Between preparing, I began to make appearances as Miss South Carolina. I was working very hard but having a ball.

Joe and Gail had asked me to move in with them, and I was so grateful to them. Gail was also one of my chaperones, and we became instant friends. Joe was like a big papa bear, and they had a son, Joey, my age. Their home offered a warm, loving atmosphere which I grew to love. My room was upstairs, with lovely white curtains and bedspread and pink flowers throughout. I guessed I would never be able to see pink flowers or the color pink without thinking of Shari.

The first weekend following my crowning, Gail and I traveled down to the coast for the Beaufort Water Festival. I was to be the mistress of ceremonies and featured vocalist for the

Miss South Carolina preliminary pageant that night. As I sang the final note of "Amazing Grace," the hot and exhausted audience stood to their feet. I was stunned at their receptiveness to a hymn, but I felt they knew it was truly my story, kind of like a theme song. The next Sunday would be my first church appearance, where I would sing and give my testimony.

Flat Rock Baptist Church was the place. Joe and Gail were members there. Gail helped me prepare the entire week, and as I stood before the congregation, I prayed for strength and the right words that would bring glory to God. I'd sung in church all my life, but I'd never had to speak for any length of time. The minister wasn't even going to preach that day, but he was giving me his entire time. I was quite nervous as I emotionally began to tell my story of the previous year. I looked out across the sea of faces, and I saw that some of them too were crying. We seemed to share a common bond in that little church that day. Several times I had to stop and regain my composure before I could continue, but I felt as if God's hand held me the whole way through that very difficult service.

No song could be more appropriate to close my testimony than the one that had been so intermingled with the many stages of my life. "Amazing Grace" would be my theme song from that day on, for the words were my own testimony, as if it had been written just for me. Its message has never changed, although my circumstances have. I knew that its author, John Newton, had himself experienced "many dangers, toils and snares," and I felt a kinship with him as I thought over all I had experienced in my twenty-two years.

I could not have picked a more loving and kind congregation with which to share my testimony for the first time. As I concluded with my final note, they graciously stood to their feet. I could only stand there on the platform and cry, grateful to the One who deserved all the glory for what He'd done.

Those seven weeks flew by, and I was soon on my way to Atlantic City. I don't think it was all sinking in, but I knew I had a job to do once I got there, and I had to do my best.

Julie and Gail had left a few days earlier to drive the U-Haul truck with all of my gowns and the pageant personnel's clothes for the week. As I sat on the governor's plane, I had to pinch myself to make sure I wasn't dreaming. I was on my way to compete for the title of Miss America!

I loved all of my gowns. Gail was such an incredible designer, and I knew I'd have the best in the pageant. I had two walk-on gowns, one black and one white. My black one was all sequins, with appliques around the sweetheart neckline. The white gown had pearls that Celine Carpentier, the seamstress who'd brought all of Gail's designs magnificently to life, had put on by hand. The neckline and short sleeves were covered with white flowers and pearls. They were gorgeous. My parade gown was a very simple white mermaid-style dress, with silver and rhinestone appliques around the sweetheart neckline. I had a matching headpiece to wear with it. My talent gown was the same one I had worn in the Miss South Carolina and Miss Liberty Pageants and could not be improved upon as far as a Juliette dress was concerned. My gold-sequined competition gown had been covered with gold appliques and weighed fifteen pounds! My shoulders would ache by the time that night was over! I would wear the same super suit for swimsuit competition, and I had a beige hand-crocheted dress for my interview. I felt so fortunate to have such a wonderful, supportive staff, people who worked on a volunteer basis, to make sure that everything I had would be perfect.

As I arrived at the Atlantic City Convention Center, the air seemed thick with the fierceness of the competition. There were beautiful girls everywhere, and at first it was intimidating. A huge map hung on a wall with each state cut out like a puzzle, and as each contestant arrived, she was to sign her name and put her state in its place, as the press cameras flashed. How exciting it all was!

Once Rita and I checked into our lovely hotel room, we had a few days to enjoy the city before the pageant began. We went out to eat at fancy restaurants, saw Gladys Knight and the Pips in concert, and had a great time. I was so glad that Julie could be there to share it all with me. Neither one of us had ever done anything like this before in our lives, both being from small towns, and we were thrilled. But the fun ended too quickly, and it was time to get busy.

Just as in the Miss South Carolina Pageant, the rehearsals began early in the morning and ended late. But there were many more press events, press parties, interviews, and photos to be taken during and between rehearsals. The story of "the tragedy" never came up while I was interviewed, and I was grateful. It was all very exciting. By the time Wednesday rolled around, I should have been worn out, but my adrenalin gave me the extra energy I needed. My first night of competition was evening gown. I was so nervous, but I constantly prayed and claimed Philippians 4:13. I knew Mom, Dad, Robert, Nana, Julie, and many other relatives and friends would be in the audience to cheer me on in that huge auditorium, and that was an encouragement to my timid heart.

I must have rehearsed my speech a million times. *Lord,*

please help me not to panic and forget it, I prayed. I made my way onto the stage, carefully remembering my placement from the hours of rehearsal. Then I waited at the top of the stairs as the contestant before me made her final turn and walked down the runway. As I began the long descent, my heel got caught in the hem of my dress! Did the judges see me stumble? No! Good, they were still watching Miss Texas walk off. I walked as gracefully as I could up to the microphone, said my speech, did my turns, and it was over. All that worry for nothing. It had only taken a total of maybe fifteen seconds! Of course there would be no announcement for the evening gown preliminary winner, but I felt I did well.

I was glad for Thursday to arrive, even though my 5:30 wake-up call came too soon. I was ready for the talent competition. I'd get to sing my aria live with the Miss America Orchestra, and I prayed the rehearsal would go well since each contestant was allowed only two run-throughs. If I was going to win a preliminary, it would be tonight.

Back in the room after rehearsal, I saw that cards and flowers, stuffed animals and koalas, along with other thoughtful gifts continued to come. So many people were there to encourage and cheer me on. Their little notes kept me going during that long week. Julie's daily note came, saying, "Sing like an angel." We had started saying that little phrase in college to each other before any performance or competition. I hoped I would do just that and that the judges would like it.

I had to be hooked up with a wireless microphone run up through the bottom of my dress and clipped onto my ruffle. As I waited on the side of the stage, I prayed once more that God would help me to do my very best. I'd worked and prepared long and hard, and I so wanted to win this category. Once out on stage, I felt an unusual calmness as the orchestra began the thrilling introduction. As I sang, I actually enjoyed myself. I again held that high C for all it was worth, and the thunderous applause made me feel good about the job I had done. I felt that the trophy would be mine as I took my bow, motioned gratitude toward the orchestra, and hurried off stage.

The swimsuit winner was announced, and as the emcees began to read the next name, I was planning how to get down those stairs and through all the other contestants scattered in front of me. My heart was pounding as I heard, "And the talent preliminary winner for tonight's competition is . . . Kelleye Cash, Miss Tennessee!" Kelleye Cash? Miss Tennessee? None of us from South Carolina had even considered her as competition, and there she was, heading for my trophy! I no longer planned how to get down those stairs. I was trying to figure out how to trip her! I fought to hold back the tears of disappointment as we watched the winners walk the runway with their trophies.

We'd not been allowed to see or talk with any of our family or friends all during this time, and Thursday night was the time to have a little party afterwards. I didn't feel much like celebrating, but it was so good to hug those who meant so much to me. Yet, inside I felt it was all over for me as far as the Miss America crown was concerned. Friday night, the final night of competition until the televised final competition, was hopeless. I'd done well in my local and state pageants by miraculously winning the swimsuit trophy, but at Miss America? No way. All I could hope for was to do a good job. I'd spent hours doing aerobics, working out with Nautilus weights, riding the stationary bike, and all those painful things to get into the best possible shape.

Once again, as I had done every night, I prayed that God would help me do my best. I made it through swimsuit competition fine, since it was the simplest of all. As we stood in our places in our closing gowns, I just wanted them to hurry up and call the names so we could get it over with and get to bed.

"For the first time in the history of the Miss America Pageant," Gary Collins was saying, "we have a tie in the swimsuit preliminary. The winners are Kelleye Cash, Miss Tennessee, and Dawn Elizabeth Smith, Miss South Carolina!"

What? I couldn't have heard him right! I couldn't believe it. Once again, it was a miracle. After all, I was only five feet, two and one-half inches tall, practically the shortest one there, with very skinny calves. No matter how many calf exercises Jack had made me do, it was hopeless. I was to forever be pencil legs! But somehow the judges must have missed that! If Shari could have seen me! She would've been as surprised as I was! I was grinning from ear to ear as Kelleye and I walked that long, historic runway. Now a renewed surge of hope began to grow within me, and I felt my dream of again walking that runway on the next night with a crown on my head might not be impossible after all.

Saturday was the longest day of the entire week. We had to have the final TV rehearsal, and we could not leave the auditorium at all. I was exhausted, and I was tired of doing the production numbers over and over and over for the television crew to get just the right shots. But the excitement of the evening ahead of me kept me going. How I hoped I'd be one of the top ten finalists. I'd worked so hard, as had every other girl there, but somehow I felt my situation was different. I'd been through so much in the last year, and I wanted to be an encouragement to other people in the country, and possibly the world, who'd also been through tragedies. I wanted to be a Miss America who could make a difference.

Joe and Gail had received the list of the top ten late that afternoon. They told me that if I'd made it, they'd be in their usual seats, and if not, they'd stay at the hotel and watch it on TV. I had to sneak a glance out from behind the side curtain. I had to know if I would be able to perform that night. Where were they? They were nowhere to be seen. My heart sank. I'd so hoped that winning a swimsuit preliminary award would have gotten me in there. I still held on to the hope that they could be running late, which wasn't at all surprising with Gail. Just before the curtain was to go up, I peeked out just once more. There they were! I began gesturing to them, pointing to myself. Gail just sat there and laughed. Well, it was show time. I'd know soon enough.

I could hardly stand the tension. Everyone looked so beautiful. As we stood on the side of the stage, I thought back just a few hours earlier to the time Jim Leone and I had in the room where he had done my hair. He kept saying that he felt that this would be the last time he'd be doing my hair and that when he said good-bye to go join the audience, that it would be the last time. He really believed I would be Miss America. He was always so genuinely encouraging. How I prayed he was right!

As the orchestra began the overture, the giddy chatter of the other contestants let me know it was finally time. I breathed a prayer, and we were on. The auditorium was packed! The room sparkled with fancy evening gowns and spotlights while camera crews worked to get every shot just as we'd rehearsed them. There they were! Joe and Gail in their box, along with the many other Miss South Carolina Pageant personnel, including Bob Pitts, first vice-president and producer, and good ole Pete Petropoulos, second vice-president and director. I finally found Julie, Mom, Dad, Robert, Nana, and so many other family members and friends throughout the enormous crowd. The excitement of seeing their beaming faces and waves as I passed by them on the runway overcame me. I was on top of the world! As we sang "Tomorrow Is Yours," I could only imagine what tomorrow would be like if I were crowned Miss America.

All in our places, we were about to hear the top ten. I was literally shaking. I kept looking over at Gail, raising my eyebrows for her to give me a hint, but she'd only smile. She was too far away for me to be able to tell anyway, I told myself.

Susan Aiken, the reigning Miss America from Mississippi, was introduced, and the audience stood to their feet as she made her way down that long runway. Then emcee Gary Collins began to tell the audience about the Miss America program's more than $200,000 in scholarships awarded each year—the largest scholarship program in the world for women. Finally he pulled the list out of his pocket. This was it. "Our top ten finalists are about to be named," he said theatrically.

It was amazing to think that out of 80,000 young women who compete each year on the local level, narrowed down to fifty-one from each state, that it was about to be narrowed down to only ten. *Please, God,* I prayed silently. How I wanted to win. *Please give me that chance.* "Our top ten finalists, who will compete all over again, one of whom will be the new Miss America are . . . Julianne Smith, Miss Virginia! Marlesa Ball, Miss Georgia! Kelleye Cash, Miss Tennessee! Kimberly McGuffie, Miss Mississippi! Angela Callahan, Miss Alabama!"

I couldn't stand it. Five names had already been called, and mine wasn't included. I started to panic, but I kept my fake smile plastered on my face. *Please, God.* Gary Collins continued, "Stephanie Samone, Miss Texas! Julie Russell, Miss Arkansas!" Seven names! Had I done that badly in every other phase of competition that my swimsuit trophy wouldn't even carry enough weight to get me in there? Surely I had high points in talent, didn't I? Only three more to go. I couldn't stand it!

"Dawn Elizabeth Smith, Miss South Carolina!" *Thank you, Lord,* I breathed, as I made my way to my place in line. "Kelly Lynn Garver, Miss Michigan! And Tamara Tungate, Miss Missouri! There they are, ladies and gentlemen, our top ten finalists!" And we were quickly whisked off the stage to get into our swimsuits for the first phase of competition. The commercial break was just around two minutes, and we had to hurry. I claimed again Philippians 4:13 as I changed. *Lord, I prayed silently, help me do my very best tonight, and if it's Your will for me to win, let it be. If not, give me the grace to accept it.*

By the time it was my turn to do my aria, it was well after 11:00 P.M., but my adrenalin was pumping full force. I prayed God would give my voice strength like never before. Quickly I'd gotten into my talent gown, placed the headpiece in place, and dashed to the side of the stage where I had to get my wireless microphone hooked through my dress and onto my belt. Julie Russell was almost finished with her talent, and I still wasn't hooked up! I started to panic, but just as Julie was making her way off stage, the stagehands finished getting me wired up. *Here I go,* I thought, as I made my way to center stage.

I gave it my all, and then we went on to the evening gown

phase. The competition was actually over. After this commercial break, the new Miss America would be crowned. I couldn't stand the suspense. I felt I had truly done my best and hoped that the judges had chosen me. It was up to them, but I knew God was ultimately in control. As the ten of us stood in line hand in hand with the other forty-one contestants behind us after the finale, I felt blessed to have even made it as far as I had. Yet I hoped for more. I'd gone there to win.

Susan Aiken made her final official walk as Miss America. "The moment has arrived," Gary Collins began. "Miss America 1987 is about to be named!" Would it be me? Somehow I couldn't fathom that I could actually be Miss America, but here I was, standing on the stage on national television as a contender.

"Our fourth runner-up and winner of a $6,000 scholarship is . . . ," he said as the drum rolled in sync with my heartbeat. *Please don't let it be me,* I said, *not yet.* "Tamara Tungate, Miss Missouri!" Graciously she stepped forward, but we all knew she was disappointed.

"The third runner-up and winner of an $8,000 scholarship is . . ." *Not me.* "Kelleye Lynn Garver, Miss Michigan!" Both girls to my right were now gone, in order. Surely the order wouldn't continue in line. I didn't want to be second runner-up like all the other times. *No, not yet,* I silently told Gary Collins.

"The second runner-up and winner of an $11,000 scholarship is . . ." *NO, please, NOT YET.* "Dawn Elizabeth Smith, Miss South Carolina!" I stepped forward, received Susan Aiken's hug, and continued to smile, but inside I was crying.

"Our first runner-up and winner of a $17,000 scholarship and . . ." Gary went on to tell how, if the new Miss America was not able to fulfill her duties for any reason that the first runner-up would become Miss America. I no longer cared, but I continued to smile. "Julianne Smith, Miss Virginia!" She seemed thrilled, and I couldn't understand why. It was killing me to have come so close, but not close enough.

"The moment has arrived," Gary said. "It's time to crown our new Miss America 1987, and here she is . . . the winner of a $30,000 scholarship . . ." We all knew who it was. The other five top ten finalists turned their heads to look at her. It was all over. "Kelleye Cash, Miss Tennessee!"

Immediately the orchestra began the introduction, and Gary was singing, "There she is, Miss America! There she is, your ideal!" She wasn't my ideal. What I'd feared had happened. All that week I'd refused to think of her as any real competition. After all, Gail had embedded into my brain that my toughest competitor would be myself, so I'd kept that attitude. But I knew that since Kelleye had been the only double preliminary winner, it was very likely that she might walk away with the crown. As she continued to make her way down the world-famous runway confidently tearless, I remembered her coming out of the judges' interview room while I had been waiting for my turn. She had clapped her hands together and said how great it went. She definitely was confident. My interview had been tough, and I had been less happy with the cold and unfriendly judges and their questions.

I fought to hide my hurt and disappointment. Kelleye Cash was Miss America, and I was second runner-up. It was over, and I just wanted to get out of there.

The awards ball followed, and as the court of honor was introduced, I continued to hold back my true feelings. The audience applauded as each of the ten finalists and runners-up were introduced, and we made our way to our tables where family and friends waited. The disappointment on the faces around my table was more than I could take. They were disappointed not in me, but with me. Joe and Gail stood to hug me and tell me how proud they were of me, and then Mom and Dad, Robert, Julie, Nana, Rita, and other pageant officials from South Carolina. Joe's face wore an angry expression. "You were robbed," he said defiantly.

We all stood to our feet as the new Miss America made her way to the podium. I forced myself to clap with everyone else. I had so wanted to be where she was. The tears began to trickle from my eyes, and I tried to no avail to stop them. As we sat down, I placed my trophy on the table in front of me. I prayed that no one else could tell I was crying, but I knew they could, as I discreetly wiped the tears away. My dream had shattered, and I was crushed.

17

LITTLE DID I REALIZE THAT NIGHT IN ATLANTIC CITY THAT GOD was trying to teach me a very important lesson. I had not been listening to Him carefully. We may not receive what we've asked for or what we think we should have, but God always gives us exactly what's best for us, what will ultimately conform us to the image of His Son, as painful as it may seem at times. And His answers are always better than the ones we would choose ourselves. Of course, at that point I could only see that I had failed. I had just known it was going to happen, and then it didn't. That disappointment joined with the greater pain of not having my sister with me.

All through that tough week I had struggled to remain positive under such tremendous pressure, but the painful memory of Shari was constantly aching in my heart. I felt somehow set apart from the rest of the contestants, that I was different from them because of what I'd been through. They were all there with pure excitement and anticipation, while my enthusiasm always held a shadow over it. But, as in most cases, God had different plans than I did.

As we silently flew back to Greenville, SC, I dreaded stepping off the plane and meeting the press, knowing I would have to come across as cheerful. I didn't feel cheerful, but we were landing. So I plastered on my fake smile and emerged with my two trophies which, to me, clearly announced to all waiting to greet their Miss South Carolina that I had not won. The cameras flashed, the questions were asked. I said something about being disappointed not only for myself, but for the entire state of South Carolina, that I was ready to get on with the year, and I was glad to finally be heading back home. I just wanted to have a large pepperoni pizza all to myself and then hibernate for a week! The many phone calls from friends and the press made that next to impossible—the hibernation, that is. My spirits were low. I honestly didn't want to look ahead to a year as Miss South Carolina. I had never planned on this. I was supposed to have been Miss America.

As I restlessly rambled down the stairs in my sweats and bedroom shoes, without a trace of make-up on and my hair in a ponytail, I was glad to finally have a day off from pictures and interviews. Joe mentioned something about what a wonderful year I was going to have, and I nonchalantly acknowledged him as I headed to the kitchen for a snack. Little did I know that he and Gail had been talking about what they could do to boost my spirits. Those two were always up to something, and that something usually meant helping somebody else.

"Dawn, how would you like to do a tape?" he asked.

"A tape? What are you talking about, Joe?"

"You could be the first Miss South Carolina ever to have her own album. What do you think?" His eyes gleamed with delight.

"I'd love it! Are you serious? How? Where? When?" I couldn't hold in my excitement.

A few weeks later, there I was in the Southeastern Sounds

Recording Studio in Easley, cutting my first record! I couldn't believe it! I'd only been in a studio a couple of times before when I'd done a few commercial jingles during college. Doing my own tape was something I'd only dreamed about. In one long and sleepless weekend, with appearances in between, and for the low, low price of just $2,500, *Dawn of a New Day* was completed. I felt so proud. I could hardly wait the six weeks it would take the tape duplicators in Nashville to finish it. Joe and Gail had helped me pick out the songs. I did "Amazing Grace," of course, "How Great Thou Art," "The Lord's Prayer," "The Day He Wore My Crown," and six others that I loved singing. The *Easley Progress* and *The Liberty Monitor* even came over and did a story about the recording while we were in the studio. Talk about getting it on the radio and into bookstores lifted my spirits quickly.

I had no idea that my year as Miss South Carolina would be such a busy one. I would make more than 350 appearances during my reign, the busiest Miss South Carolina ever up to that point. And the people of the state didn't seem to care that I was just Miss South Carolina and second runner-up, as they kindly told me that I was *their* Miss America. The dear people of my home state knew well what my family and I had been through. They seemed to be celebrating my victories right along with me. Practically everywhere I went, people recognized me, and so many of those people were Christians. Hundreds would tell me how they had prayed for my family during the horrible ordeal. God had heard their prayers, and I knew that each of them had a part in bringing us through.

There were grand openings where ribbons had to be cut and autographs given, dinners and luncheons at which I would entertain, civic clubs where I would speak, pageants I would emcee, parades to ride in, and countless other places where I was to "appear." Festivals, schools, receptions, and charitable organizations, such as Easter Seals and the March of Dimes, asked me to be their spokesperson. I sang "Amazing Grace" at the Honorable Governor Carroll Campbell's inauguration. But as special as each was, my favorites were the ones that God planned for me.

Although I had not actually decided to recommit myself to full-time Christian service, it was as if God was putting me right where He wanted me. Churches by the hundreds continued to call my business manager, and I even began to give concerts in churches in South Carolina. Eventually I crossed the state lines into North Carolina and Georgia. I was amazed at the doors God opened. As I painfully shared the part of my life that had been so tragic, I began to see how God was taking it, with all of its ugliness and loss, and turning it into something beautiful for His glory. At the same time, I was beginning to heal. So many hurting people, who'd also experienced tragedies and lost loved ones unexpectedly, would come up to me after the services and hug me, telling me how much it meant to hear me share how God's grace had brought me through and that it was there for them, too. I could never have guessed that this much good could possibly come from the loss we had experienced. Yet the words from Shari's own "last will and testament" letter were becoming more real to me with each passing day. God began to show me that what He had brought me through could really make a difference in other people's lives, if I'd only share it. As Shari had put it, "Everything works out for the good for those that love the Lord." Those words began to ring as true as a crystal clear bell within my heart.

I continued to live with the Sanders. Gail chaperoned me about 99 percent of the time, and she and I shared experiences that neither one of us will ever forget. Most of that year we spent in the car and in hotel rooms, driving from one town to the next, with lots of laughter and very little sleep in between. We soon became close friends, and I will always cherish that special year that Gail sacrificed to travel with me when she could have been doing a million and one other things. Gail and I spent many of those long hours in the car talking about Shari, her fun-loving personality and how much we all missed her. Gail began to encourage me to write a book about it. God used her listening ear and understanding heart greatly in my own life as I continued to put the pieces of my life back together. Yet I knew in my heart I had not healed enough to be able to relive and write down on paper what I had experienced. The wounds were still too fresh.

We ate a lot of fast food, but when we were home, she, Joe, and Joey knew where we had to go on Tuesday nights. It became a tradition. Tuesday night at the Pizza Inn in Easley was buffet night. None of them could believe how much pizza this five-foot, two-and-one-half, 105-pound girl could eat, but they didn't complain. It actually became a "family" joke.

One night Gail and I had to head back to Liberty after an appearance in Columbia. We hadn't been home in a while and just could not stand to stay in a hotel one more night. When we stopped to fill the gas tank, Gail told me she simply could not drive—she was too tired. The trip was unusually quiet for two women who normally never run out of things to say. When we finally made it into Mauldin, a town thirty miles from Liberty, we both were about to fall asleep. It was the dead of winter, and Gail had her window halfway down, trying to stay awake. I was so exhausted that I could no longer hold in my frustrations. I began to cry, telling Gail that there was no way I would be able to get up early the next morning to make it to yet another appearance. I looked at Gail to see if she'd even heard me! She hadn't said a word.

"Gail!" I demanded.

Slowly she looked over at me from the passenger's side and wearily said, "Dawn, save it. Save it for somebody who can help you. I'm too tired."

We finally made it home, dragged ourselves and our suitcases up the stairs, and woke Joe up. He thought we were crazy, of course, as we complained of exhaustion and burnout. He thought I had really lost it when I asked him if he could just call the place where I was supposed to be the next day and tell them I was sick.

"Dawn, Miss South Carolina just doesn't call in sick! You can't do that to those people. They're expecting you to be there," he said in his fatherly voice.

I knew Gail felt no more like going than I did. She said that all the way on that miserable two-hour trip, all she could do was pray that she would not die before we made it back to Liberty. She knew I was too tired to be able to handle that! With that, we all were in the middle of the bed in stitches!

I still had to repack. The alarm would ring at 3:30 because I needed to catch a 5:30 flight to Maryland for a girls' retreat where I was to speak and sing for the weekend. I still wanted to call in sick. I felt sick, I was so tired. As I began to pack, I had to look deep within myself and ask just why I was doing all this. Was it because it was my responsibility as Miss South Carolina and I really had no other choice? Or was there really more to it? I felt God was speaking to my heart as He brought

to mind the verse I had been sharing wherever I went—
Philippians 4:13, "I can do all things through Christ who
strengthens me." Wow. Did I really believe that? Did I really
practice what I preached? I knew there would be many more
nights like this one. As the sobering reality hit me in the wee
hours of that dark night, with no piano around, I wrote my
first song. It was a simple chorus, with just two verses and a
bridge. I was finished in about fifteen minutes, with both the
words and melody. I pounded into Gail's room to quietly sing
her the song while Joe slept.

As I wake up every morning with another day ahead,
I sometimes wish I didn't have to get out of bed!
I wonder what the purpose is for all the things I do.
Then You gently re-remind me, my purpose is You!

CHORUS
And because of You,
I can do all things with the strength You give.
Because of You,
I have no questions as to why I live,
and because of You,
I can smile when I'm feeling sad and blue.
Oh, Lord, it's all because of You!

The days seem long, yet time's so short, and it seems to never end.
Running here and there and everywhere, I think it's more than I
    can stand.
Then I feel so very foolish when I realize the price
that You paid for me at Calvary, so that I could have this life.

You put the sun in the midst of clouds.
You give assurance where there is doubt.
You give me hope in each new day.
So in Your love is where I'll stay!

"Because of You" was an instant hit with Joe and Gail, and I could hardly wait to get to a piano and pick it out. It seemed I learned lessons only when I was at the end of my rope, forced to look to God. I had been preaching well on living out Philippians 4:13, but the Lord wanted me to probe deeply into my own heart and make sure I was living it, not just in the tragedies, but in the everyday, sometimes mundane, hustle and bustle of life as well. I knew that without the strength I'd found in Him, I could not have come out of the depths of desperation, fear, and grief. I also knew very well that His grace is truly sufficient for our every need, no matter what our circumstance. I had to get on my knees that night and thank Him for re-reminding me of that great truth.

Christmas was a wonderful time, with over fifteen parades to ride in, many of them in freezing rain. A bad case of bronchitis followed. Somehow, though, I made it through. It snowed not long after, and the blanket of white was a welcome surprise. A South Carolina snow is pretty unusual, and I could hardly wait to get out in it. Joey and I went right to work, not on any old snowman, but on a "snow queen." She was beautiful—crown and all! She had her own scarf, carrot nose, button eyes, red lips, and the Miss South Carolina crown. We had to get a picture of that! With the snow came a much-needed break, spent riding cookie sheets and garbage can lids down the hill in the back yard with Joey and his cousins. Indoors, Gail greeted us with her homemade vegetable soup. Memories of younger days and snowmen from the big snow we had in the '70s warmed my heart.

My twenty-third birthday came. The year was coming to a close. The Billy Graham Crusade would soon be held in Columbia, SC, and Joe and Gail began to talk about trying to get me on the program. I felt it was impossible. But they knew Cliff Barrows, who also lived upstate, and soon, to my dismay, I was to be a part of the crusade! At first I was only going to share a brief testimony. But Gail would not have it. She was determined that I would sing, not just any song, but my song. However, there just wasn't enough time in the service that night, and the music had already been planned.

Gail was not one to give up easily. As we scurried around in our hotel room that afternoon with the local Christian radio station playing, the announcers promoted the service for that night and mentioned my name! Then, to our shock, he played one of my songs from *Dawn of a New Day!* I was on the radio!

Then the phone rang, and I answered it. It was Cliff Barrows's secretary. I knew what she was calling about—it just could not be worked out to have me sing.

"Dawn," she began, "we would really like you to sing a verse or two of 'Amazing Grace' at the conclusion of your testimony."

I couldn't thank her enough. Gail, Julie, and I jumped up and down like schoolgirls. I prayed again, as I had so many times before, that God would give me strength, the words He would have me say, and the power of His Holy Spirit as I shared. Then it was time to go.

The stadium was almost packed. There must have been

sixty thousand people! What in the world was I doing there? I'd had the privilege of singing for First Baptist Church of Houston's Easter service where there had been around nine thousand. I'd traveled to Virginia to be on the "700 Club," but this crowd was, to say the least, overwhelming for this little girl from Red Bank, SC. As Mom, Dad, Gail, and I made our way up onto the platform, I saw Dr. Graham coming toward us. I felt honored to meet him, much less be on the same platform with him. What an incredible difference his ministry had made in the world. I admired him so much.

I was so nervous I could hardly stand it. Cliff Barrows led the crowd in singing several hymns, the choir and soloists sang, and then it was my time to share. The crusade band and I had been able to go over the song only one time. We were going to do the first, third, and last verses. *Oh, God,* I prayed, *I know it's only Your grace that has gotten me here; I lean on that as I stand before this enormous crowd.* Soon I had finished my testimony and was singing the final note of my song. The people stood to their feet before I could even finish. I could not stop my tears as I made my way back to my seat. Mom, Dad, and Gail were wiping them away, too. That, for me, had been a dream come true. I sat in awe at the grace of God as we listened, only a few feet away, while Dr. Billy Graham preached that night, and the people came forward in droves. It was a thrill and an honor I'd never experienced before—to be a small part of something so awesome. God's grace was truly amazing to me.

And I realized more than ever just how much I depended on God's grace. Right in the middle of the most exciting year of my life, the Helmick case went to trial, and I had to testify. Larry Gene Bell had crossed my mind many times, but I always tried to push those thoughts away and dwell on more positive things. As I walked into the courthouse again, it looked just like the one in Berkeley County. The memories of our own trial, which I had buried deep, began to surface. How I dreaded to see him again. But I wanted to help insure that he would receive justice. My heart went out to the Helmick family as I saw them sitting up on the front row, just as we'd done. Their other children were so young. It was all so unfair. I'd seen so much good in the world over the last year, so much good that had come out of my own tragedy, and yet good was hard to find in that room that day.

Gail and I met Mom and Dad outside the double doors that led to the courtroom, the familiar nervousness rising in me as my time to testify drew nearer. There Bell was, looking just as I'd remembered him. Again it seemed prison life must not have been too hard; he'd gained more weight.

I prayed there would be no more outbursts or crazy statements directed toward me this time. I wanted to get this over quickly. My part was simple. All I had to do was testify to the fact that he had called our home and given me the directions to Debra's body. I had to identify the voice on the tape as Bell's. As I spoke, he didn't even look up at me. Yet as I made my way out of the witness box, our eyes met. I quickly turned and was seated next to Mom, Dad, and Gail. My parents were there to show support for the Helmicks.

As we sat in the pews of that old dusty room, I could feel the stares of people. I felt so odd being there. This was certainly not one of my appearances, but the people just kept staring and whispering. They saw me as so many others did, as Dawn Smith, Miss South Carolina, Shari Smith's sister. *How insensitive,* I thought. The woman in front of us kept turning around as if she wanted to say something, but I continued to look straight ahead.

"Dawn," she finally whispered, "I watched you on the Miss America Pageant and just knew you were going to win. Can I get your autograph?" She reached to hand me a pen and a piece of paper over the back of the pew.

I was annoyed at the inappropriate request. I said something about it not being the time or place, as I caught a look of disbelief from Mom. I didn't care. I was not about to sign an autograph in the middle of a murder trial.

Larry Gene Bell received his second death penalty sentence, and I breathed a prayer of gratitude. Now I was certain he'd never get out again.

●

July was just around the corner, and the stark realization that I would no longer be Miss South Carolina suddenly hit me. I had been so consumed with the incredible experiences of a reigning state queen that I really hadn't thought about it ending. As Dad had put it, I was about to enter the "real world." And to be quite honest, it scared me.

Of course, during my competition, I had talked about pursuing a Masters degree in vocal performance at Indiana University, but somehow I could not feel peace about doing that. I knew that nothing would make Joe and Gail or Mrs. Palmer any happier, but deep inside, I just couldn't. I knew what I felt God wanted me to do, but had no idea if it was even possible. I wanted to continue to sing for the Lord, but I was afraid no one would call me once I became a "has-been." Yet it was what I'd committed my life to, God had brought me this far, and I'd just have to trust Him to continue what He'd started.

Finally I made my last official walk as Miss South Carolina with the audience on their feet in that historic Greenville Memorial Auditorium. I could not help crying as my farewell speech was played and I walked the ramp the last time. I wanted all there that night, as well as those watching on television across the state, to know that I gave all the glory to my Savior, Jesus Christ. So for my final words of farewell, I sang my testimony, "Amazing Grace." My voice quivered with emotion through several parts of that beautiful song, but I felt the strength of God upon me and knew His message still rang out loudly and clearly. Another chapter of my life had closed . . . a very special one that I will always be deeply grateful for and remember from time to time with a smile, a laugh, and a tear. But it was once again time to move on.

18

TO MY DELIGHT, PEOPLE DID CONTINUE CALLING ME TO SING, AND 1987 was just as busy as 1986 had been. God had launched me in the ministry He had planned for my life from the platform of Miss South Carolina. With the scholarship money I'd received, I was able to record my second tape, *Dawn*, in Nashville, with "Because of You" as the opening song. I was having the time of my life. Life did go on after the pageant. God had granted me the privilege not only to represent the state of South Carolina during that special year, but He'd granted me an even greater honor that would continue for the rest of my life—the privilege of representing Him in this world.

The year 1988 came, and the doors continued to open. I began to travel outside South Carolina into other states in the southeast. God continued to use my testimony and music ministry in ways beyond what I could have imagined. I had lost a sister, yet so many other people, both men and women, could relate to my situation and find encouragement.

Dad and Mom still continued in their business and with their various ministries. Dad served as a chaplain for the Lexington County Jail. He held a Bible study weekly at a boys' correctional school. Mom and Dad together worked with an organization entitled C-STOP, and Mom ministered at the women's prison facility. Along with so many other people, I was amazed at what they were doing. Only by the grace of God could they minister to the very type of person who had killed their beloved daughter.

Robert was about to graduate from Lexington High School, which I found hard to believe. He was on the principal's honor roll and had received many basketball awards. My little brother would be attending Newberry College on a basketball scholarship, and I was so proud of him. There he was second in the state in the three-point shoot, and he continued to make the dean's list. Even after the storm, we each found that, as difficult as it is, life does go on.

And Larry Gene Bell continued to wait on death row.

We decided it was time to think about doing another recording, as my ministry continued to extend beyond the southeast. I had sung several times for a program called "First Love," which was nationally televised on the American Christian Television Satellite Network by the First Baptist Church of Columbia. I had met the program's producer, Kevin McAfee, on the set that year. I developed a friendship with him and his family and the folks at First Baptist and soon became a member-in-residence.

Kevin encouraged me to keep writing music as we worked on finding the songs to record. This would be my first all-original album project. During the next three months, with my scholarship money again funding the project, we decided upon eleven songs and came up with the title, *Hosanna Forever*. In May we began recording in Key of Life Studios in Columbia, and Kevin co-produced with the owner, Gary Davis. Ironically, we recorded the song, "Sisters," which I'd

written in memory of Shari, on the three-year anniversary of
her death. I had only to sing it a few times, and the words and
music once again gave me hope.

Sister

written by Dawn Smith Jordan (and Phillip Sandifer)
(in memory of Shari)

Beautiful at seventeen, full of hope and plans
The future seemed so bright to you
The world was in your hands
But in an instant you were gone
Taken far from me
The pain and the senseless loss
Were all that I could see

"Was this really happening?" I asked in disbelief
And though there were no answers
In Jesus there was peace
This separation that we know is only for a while
For if He truly conquered death
We truly never die

CHORUS

The friendship, joy, and dreams we shared
Won't even begin to compare
To the time when we're together again.
The bond we have in Jesus love
Will always keep us
Together, forever, sister

Sister, you're a precious gift God chose to lend to me
The priceless love that you have shared
Is one that never leaves
Now your life is in His hands
And even death will bow
Eternity will dry the tears
I'm cryin for you now

Performed by Dawn Smith Jordan, 1993 Urgent Music recording "Canopy" ©
1995 234 Music/BMI, Urgent Music Group, P.O. Box 90754 Austin, TX 78709
(512) 282-4036

The entire album I dedicated to Shari in loving memory. The project was completed, and I began using it in my concert ministry everywhere the Lord sent me.

About that time, Kevin kept telling me about this guy he thought would be just perfect for me. I'd heard that before and was NOT interested! But he would not give up. He told me Will Jordan was good-looking and 100 percent committed to Christ. A student at the University of South Carolina, Will was currently serving as an intern with the Student Ministries there at the church. But I was very busy with my ministry, and I wasn't ready to date again. I'd just broken up a long relationship and needed a break.

In August, however, Will Jordan and I went out on our first date. That night when we went to dinner and to a movie, I remembered that I had seen him at Lexington Baptist Church a few years before. To my surprise, I actually had a great time. Will was the perfect gentleman. He'd even brought me flowers when I came to the door. He had decided to let me get to know the real Will right off the bat. Instead of borrowing his father's car, he picked me up in his '77 Chevrolet Blazer. I liked that.

We went out again, and again. On the third date, as we sat on the couch just before he was to leave that evening, he asked if we could pray together for the city-wide crusade in Tulsa, Oklahoma, with Dr. John Bisagno. I would be singing at the crusade the next week. We awkwardly held hands, as it was customary to do in both of our families. As he began to pray, something inside me—I believe it was the Spirit of the Lord—told me that this was the man I would marry. I had no doubts. Right then and there I was ready to propose to him, but I thought it might be better to let him do that. That night I could hardly sleep. I'd met the very man God had planned for me.

In Tulsa I could no longer keep it to myself, so I called Mom from my hotel room. She thought I was absolutely crazy when I asked her what she thought about a June wedding. After all, that would give us ten months! I bought my first *Bride* magazine and began dreaming about my wedding. I felt pretty sure that Will felt the same way about me. Our phone bill during that nine days we were apart was sky high, but I still needed to hear him say it.

In the meantime, we were discovering all about each other. Will told me how he had come to know the Lord, and I knew he was a man who loved God with all of his heart. I had found a gem. He had grown up in a strong Christian home. But like most teens, he had given in to peer pressure to "fit in" with the crowd. As a result, he had developed a serious problem with alcohol and drugs during high school and college.

Money, success, and prestige became paramount in Will's life. To support his lifestyle, he had turned to drug trafficking in Columbia. In 1983, he was arrested for possession and distributing drugs. For that he was kicked out of school. Everything that had been important to him was being stripped away. Will was placed in a pre-trial intervention program by the state as an alternative to actually serving time in prison. Completing this program erased his arrest record. But something was still missing. His heart and life needed cleaning as well.

Will finally realized that what he had heard from his parents and church was true—that he really had nothing without God. Longing for the cleansing and the purpose that Jesus offers, Will asked the Lord to come into his life. The Lord went to work immediately, transforming Will into a new person. Two years later, he returned to college, and in 1989, he received a Bachelor's degree in business management from the University of South Carolina. The prayers of his mother and father, Bill and Carol Jordan, had been answered after five long years. And my prayers were answered as well.

I waited for two long, long weeks to hear those three little words. And finally they came. Will found a really creative way to propose to me. I was ill with a fever and bronchitis, home on the couch, when he came over to my apartment on a Saturday night after a youth rally he'd helped lead. He said he'd gotten me some candy and had also called Mike McKenzie, a friend of ours who was a doctor, to get me some medicine. I immediately went for the candy.

After about thirty minutes, Will said that he thought I'd better start my medication. I noticed he was a little nervous. I looked at the prescription. The name on the bottle was "Dawn Jordan." I asked Will what in the world that meant, and he said something about Mike just playing a trick on us since we were so in love. As I read on, I knew something was going on.

"Take one tablet per lifetime for divine happiness." What? I was afraid to open it. Will's beautiful blue-green eyes were sparkling as he tried to hide his excitement. There, on the top of the cotton inside the little bottle, was the most beautiful engagement ring I'd ever seen! He'd gotten me just what I'd hoped for—a perfect oval diamond. Tears filled my eyes as he asked me if I'd marry him, and I said yes over and over as we hugged and kissed. Although I had to cancel a concert I was supposed to have had the next day out of town, nothing was going to keep me from making it to church the next morning. I had to show the world, fever or not! I had truly found "God's perfect *Will*" for my life. Kevin was feeling greatly successful as Cupid; he was so full of himself.

In the midst of the excitement, something unexpected occurred. I was still learning to live with the tragedy that had so affected every aspect of my life. So many questions remained unanswered about Shari's kidnapping and murder. Why did Bell take Shari, and why did he have to kill her? Why didn't she run away from him toward the house as Dad had always taught us to? Did he really have a gun? How did she really die? Did she suffer? Was she really not afraid at all? There were many days when I thought about going to Larry Bell's cell and asking him what really happened, but I knew that would be impossible. Besides, I couldn't trust his word.

Part of Kevin's duties at the church were pastoral in nature. He worked in the college department and often was involved in missions and ministries for the church. One afternoon in the middle of the summer in 1988, Bob McAlister, deputy chief-of-staff for the governor, invited Kevin to minister at the Columbia Correctional Institute. The chaplain and several laymen from Columbia with an organization called Prison Fellowship held a weekly chapel service on death row.

Bob was going to pick Kevin up at the church on this particular Tuesday and for some reason did not show up. Kevin waited. Finally thinking he had gotten his signals mixed up, he drove several blocks from downtown to the prison. He stopped at the gate and told the guard he was supposed to meet Bob McAlister from Governor Campbell's staff, and the guard opened up the prison fence. Kevin drove the Astro mini-van through the dual set of wired gates.

When he went to the first prison door, one cell door opened and closed behind him, as the security system regulated all traffic, especially visitors. The officer asked him why he was there, and once again Kevin told his story. Then he was ushered through the open jail to Cell Block III—death row. The sounds were loud and hauntingly ominous as the doors once again opened and closed several times with a single officer leading him through.

All the prisoners were in blue jeans. They were very aware that a visitor was in the yard. After going through several more doors, Kevin was met by an officer who asked him to sign in and said, "Chapel for the row is at the end of the hall; Bob is probably down there. Don't get close to the doors."

Kevin had to walk past twenty or so cells to get to the chapel location. He was unescorted when he walked by the cells of men waiting to die. At the end of the hall a group of thirty or forty prisoners were singing "Swing Low, Sweet Chariot," and they were having a church service.

The room was about fifteen feet by fifteen feet, and most of the men were sitting on the floor or the wooden benches. There was nothing about this assortment of men—intellectuals, illiterates, blacks, whites, Indians—that would identify them as murderers.

Kevin sat down on the floor and was handed a song sheet by one of the inmates. The worship was in full swing. Some of the inmates sang solos, shared stories, and Bible verses.

The chaplain then asked if anyone was rejoicing in his trials. Several said they were "counting it all joy." One of the prisoners began to cry and say that he wanted to be like Jesus.

There did not appear to be a guard or anyone from the outside in this small room, and finally Kevin realized Bob McAlister was not even there. In a room full of murderers, he did not know a soul. He was extremely nervous. Only later did he find out that Bob McAlister had missed being there due to a scheduling conflict.

One by one, the prisoners began to testify of how God had been making a difference in their lives. Some prisoners even told of their salvation experience, and Kevin was deeply moved.

He left the chapel and stopped to talk to one of the prisoners in the hall just outside the chapel door. He asked this particular man why he didn't join all the others in the chapel. The inmate replied, "I was responsible for two children." An unwritten rule behind prison walls makes a convict who mistreats children a hated outcast.

Kevin asked, "What happened?"

The prisoner told him that he had been the object of the largest manhunt in the state of South Carolina. He said that he had learned a lot about God because, since he was behind bars, he had had a lot of time to think. Quoting from the fifteenth chapter of John verbatim, the prisoner clearly demonstrated that he had been reading the Bible a lot. He then proceeded to tell his story. After a few moments, Kevin realized who the man was. Larry Gene Bell was telling a story about the song, "Sisters," that Kevin had produced just a few months ago.

Kevin did not say anything to Bell about knowing me. After about fifteen minutes of questions, Kevin excused himself. He immediately returned to the church and called Bob McAlister and was amazed at what he discovered. Bob asked, "Do you mean they let you on death row without me being there? That is so unusual, and it's almost impossible you were even allowed in!"

Kevin realized that God must be at work in what was happening. He stopped by Will's office, needing someone to talk to. Kevin asked Will's advice on whether to tell me about it. A little later that day I needed to stop by the church. As I stuck my head into Kevin's office, he asked me to come in and shut the door. He began to tell me about his experience at the prison.

"Did you see him?"

"Yes," he replied.

"Did you talk to him?"

"Yes."

"What did he say to you?" I had to know.

As Kevin began to tell me, I sat mesmerized in my chair across from his desk. He hesitated before speaking as he was finding it difficult to respond. "Dawn, I had no idea Larry Gene Bell was in the Columbia Correctional Institute. I thought he had been shipped off to some other state. I didn't know I would be talking to him. Bob McAlister told me it was nothing short of a miracle the guards even let me into the prison at all."

Kevin told me that Larry Bell had said that he was a

Christian; he had accepted the Lord. Kevin wasn't sure what to believe, but Bell quoted from Psalms when he said, "You will know the wicked by their countenance."

"I saw a defeated man who had only one thing in his life, and it appeared to be God. I didn't tell him who I was or that we were even acquaintances," Kevin went on.

Larry Bell told Kevin, "I deserve to die because of what was done, but where I am going is a much better place. I'll be in Heaven."

Kevin then asked me a question I'd never been asked. "Dawn, have you forgiven him?"

Stunned, I thought for a second. Then I said, "Yes, I have, and I truly hope he is a Christian." I then began to tell Kevin about all the unanswered questions I'd had for so long. Kevin agreed that he should try to go back to the prison and ask Bell these questions.

A week passed, and when Kevin was ushered back into the prison, Bob McAlister accompanied him to the cell of Larry Bell before the scheduled Tuesday chapel service. During the past week the word had gotten to Larry through some of the volunteers—Kevin was Dawn's producer.

When the prisoner saw Kevin, he said, "I know who you are, and I've been praying for someone like you for three years to come to my cell. Before I die, would you ask Dawn and her family for forgiveness? I don't think I could even go on if I weren't able to ask this of the families who have been hurt." Bell continued, "I am ready to answer any questions you might have of me."

"What actually happened on that day in May of 1985?" Kevin asked first.

Bell referred to the "evil one" or the "other person" as he

recounted the abduction in the third person. Diagnosed as paranoid schizophrenic, he was transferring blame and talking about himself as two different people, the good one and the evil one.

He said, "Shari and I had met once before, and when the evil one drove up by the mailbox, there was no sign of struggle because she was invited into the car." Shari was such a trusting and loving person. She would have had no reason to run from someone she knew, if this was true.

Mr. Bell said that the evil one took Shari to a house and tied her up. He then talked with her for a while but said that he didn't rape her. He gave her the choice of the way she wanted to leave this earth. There was no gun involved. "Then the good person came back and tried to help her escape from the evil one, because the evil one had left the room for a while. The good person was nice to Shari and let her write her 'last will and testament.' Then when the evil one came back, he used a drug such as chloroform. She inhaled the drug from a large cotton ball he put over her face, and she went to sleep." As Kevin described this horrible ordeal, neither of us could hold back the tears.

Kevin decided to continue meeting with the man who killed my sister and the nine-year-old girl throughout the fall of the year. In connection with the chapel services on death row, Kevin prayed with many of these men. He believed that many of the inmates there had a personal relationship with Jesus Christ. We do serve a God of the second chance.

Will and Kevin would talk about the tragedy and pray together for me and also for Mr. Bell. "When you have done it unto the least of these, you have done it unto Me," were the words of Jesus. Larry Gene Bell was truly "the least of these." I knew I could not live with anger and malice in my heart.

When I told Kevin I had forgiven the man, only one thing ran through my mind—the grace of God. I didn't feel any better or worse after Kevin had told me the answers Larry Bell had given him, but at least that contact had been made. I realized that some things on this earth we may never understand and never receive the answers to, but we can trust God and His grace to carry us through those days of questions and doubts. I didn't really trust the words of a murderer, but I was thankful that God had supernaturally allowed Kevin to meet the man. I came to the stark realization that I had to accept the fact that many times we may never know why, how, what or when, but as long as we know Who, He is enough. I used to think that when I got to Heaven, I would march right up to God and ask Him all the why's and how's so that I could finally know. But now I realize that in Heaven, none of those things will matter anymore. I will only be able to fall at His feet with the utmost gratitude for the salvation He's granted me and worship Him for all eternity. All the pain and sorrow will be well worth it for just one glimpse of His beautiful face in that perfect place He's prepared for His children—where Shari is, where there is no more pain or crying.

19

SEVEN MONTHS AFTER OUR FIRST DATE, WILL AND I WERE MARRIED.
It was a beautiful ceremony. Will and I both wanted, above all
else, for Jesus to be glorified in the service.

Julie, now Mrs. Clif Caldwell, was my matron of honor.
She had been happily married for two years to a medical student from Columbia. That day she sang more beautifully than
I'd ever heard her before. There was a special flower arrangement, matching the other bridesmaids' bouquets, around the
unity candle in memory of Shari. How I wanted her there with
me on that wonderful day. Her name was listed in the program as my maid of honor in loving memory. The pain in my
heart at losing her was still very sharp, but the joy of that day
was sweeter than any I'd ever known.

Robert was the most handsome groomsman, standing six
feet, one inch in his tuxedo, grinning from ear to ear. Robert
had always told me that he just knew Will would be perfect for
me to marry, but I had never listened to him. What did my little brother know about that? I could have sworn I saw a tear
glistening in his brown-green eyes as I'd smile over at him
during the service. I knew the reason for Mom's and Dad's
tears. They were very happy for me, but I also knew the day
held a deep sadness for them. They knew this would be the

only daughter they would ever be able to give away. As much as they wanted to share in my happiness, they couldn't forget that they had hoped someday to be doing this for Shari also, and they would never have the chance. But they gave Will and me the most beautiful wedding and reception we could ever ask for, and we will always be grateful.

Among the cards and letters of congratulation, I received an unexpected piece of mail. It was from Larry Gene Bell, still on death row. He had written on a card that wished me a happy twenty-fifth birthday, and he wished Will and me much happiness in our marriage. On the back of the envelope, with the return address of "Life Row," was a little smiley face. I remembered the one that had looked so much like it—the one my precious sister had written on her "last will and testament" letter years before beside "God is love." I wondered how he'd found my address. Will and I tucked it away in a file someplace and tried to forget about it.

Not only did God give me the most wonderful godly man to spend my life with, but He blessed me with the best "in-loves" in the world—two more younger brothers, Britt and Page, and the privilege of being a big sister again—to his little sister, Caroline.

Will's grandmother, "Mema," was an added blessing. I was surprised to learn that Will's mother had grown up in Moncks Corner and that Mema still lived there. It was a Jordan tradition to spend Christmas at Mema's. The first Christmas there was strange, and each year it brings an odd feeling as we drive into the little town. The familiar buildings and surroundings still bring back those harsh memories of the month I spent there during the trial of my sister's murderer. But how like God to give me new and wonderful memories, as well, of family, celebration, and happiness in a place that once held only sadness. The memories of the trial will never go away, but now Moncks Corner is a much-loved place where special loved ones live. How I thank God for His goodness in all things. He thinks of everything.

After our marriage, at the leading of the Lord we formed Jordan Ministries, Inc., a full-time ministry committed to spreading the gospel to a lost world. God began to open doors for us to minister. Since Will has a deep love and burden for young people as well as for the local church, God began to give him opportunities to speak in youth rallies and services across the country. We shared in a concert ministry together with our testimonies and my music. What an honor to be able to travel together, sharing the greatest thing in our lives—Jesus Christ!

Not until after we were married did I realize, as we were talking one night about losing Shari and the horror of the tragedy that would forever leave a scar on my life, that Will was the other young man who had come that day years before with Mark Heckle, bringing Robert and me the pepperoni pizza. God's grace had even allowed him to be there to experience the most difficult tragedy in my life along with me, beginning that very first day when he showed up with a heart full of concern to help in the search.

Today, we stand in awe of what God has done in our lives and ministry. Neither of us would ever have believed in those dark days of tragedy that God would use us to further His kingdom. Proverbs 3:5, 6 have become my life verses: "Trust in the Lord with all your heart, and lean not on your own understanding. In all your ways acknowledge Him, and He will direct your paths." Even when I can't see past my pain, and even in the midst of those long deserts when I'm begging for rain, I know that God is there. His faithfulness has been proven to me time and time again, and I know He will never disappoint me. I don't have all the answers, but I truly don't have to. I have the one Answer who is sufficient for all things, and I know I can trust Him. As one of my favorite songs says, "When answers aren't enough, there is Jesus."

Just before Will and I were to leave Columbia in August of 1990 to move to Fort Worth, Texas, where Will would begin his studies toward a Master of Divinity at Southwestern Baptist Theological Seminary, we received another piece of mail from Bell. This time it was more than just a note. John 3:16 appeared in the corner beside "Life Row." Written on legal-sized paper, it was several pages long. I was afraid to read it at first. But as I began, I could tell it must have taken him a very long time to write. The handwriting looked like some sort of calligraphy, and it was practically all Scripture. I could not get one of the verses out of my mind: "But if you do not forgive men, then your Father will not forgive your transgressions" (Matthew 16:15 NASB). I knew that verse well, and I knew that I had forgiven Bell. At first impulse, I thought, *How dare he write me a letter like this, as if he's condemning me after what he's done.* Yet the words would not leave me alone.

As we came on to Texas, the thought of that letter was very upsetting to me. I was still not completely free. Once again, even after four years of much healing, I had those familiar feelings of anger and bitterness toward him. I had to settle it once and for all.

Little did I know that God would use the letter from the very man who had murdered my sister to change my life, again forever. I had to ask myself if I had really forgiven him. Although I really believed I had, I had never let him know that. He had no idea what I felt toward him. I knew God was speaking to me through that Scripture, asking me to write Bell.

As I sat down at my desk in our ministry office, I stared at the keys of my typewriter for what seemed an eternity. I didn't know how to begin or what to say to the man I had tried not to think about for over five years. We seldom talked about him. I felt so nervous, all alone. But I knew I wasn't really alone, that God was with me as He'd always been and that He'd give me the right words, as He'd done so many other times before.

"Dear Gene," I began. I called him Gene because that was the name he went by, the name his family and friends called him. Bob McAlister had graciously agreed to deliver the letter to him for me. It was dated March 22, 1991.

> *Hi. I know you may think it odd that I am writing to you, but I felt this is something the Lord would have me do. I had received your letter as well as the congratulations you sent to Will and me on our wedding. I feel you did these with good intentions. This letter is sent in the same way.*
>
> *Since Shari died almost six years ago, the Lord has brought me through many things—feelings of anger, fear, and numerous questions as to why this had to happen to my precious sister. Through all of my questions, one thing has been so ever present in my life, and that's God's unchanging grace to me. His grace is what has brought me to this point in my life, and it is His grace that has caused me to write this letter to you. Although I can never forget what you did to my family, I want you to know that I have forgiven you. I have*

never hated or held any feelings of hatred toward you, but it was not until now that I felt I could write this letter to you in total honesty.

You see, just as God's grace has been there for me, it is also there for you. When Jesus died on that horrible, cruel cross, He did it to cover every single one of our sins with His precious blood. The Bible says that if we accept Jesus into our lives as Savior and Lord, He casts our sins as far as the east is from the west. What a wonderful promise for us all!

I have prayed for you and your family over the last several years, and I pray that you all will somehow come to know what the Bible calls "the peace that passes all understanding." It can only come from putting ourselves in the hands of God. Because of this, I have the assurance that I will see Shari again. Just as she shared with you, God can forgive you, and so can I because of Him. As she said, and you said to me in one of our many phone conversations, "Some good will come out of this." Although this situation was not good, God has used it for His glory.

I will continue to pray for you. You are truly forgiven and never have to question that. Proverbs 3:5, 6 have become my life verses, and I'd like to leave them with you. "Trust in the Lord with all your heart, and lean not on your own understanding. In all your ways acknowledge Him, and He will direct your paths." May God bless you!

In His service,
Dawn Smith Jordan

As I sat back and read over what I'd written, I felt as if a tremendous burden had lifted. Never before had I felt such a freedom and peace within. I saw an entirely new dimension of God's powerful grace. It goes beyond all barriers to the very ones who are the offenders. After all, that's what Jesus did for us. God's perfect, blameless Son was murdered too—by my sin and yours. Yet He forgave the very ones who took His life on a cruel cross. And we are to extend His mercy and forgiveness to those who have caused us pain. For He Himself has done no less for us, as undeserving as we are. That is truly amazing grace.

Now for me I knew the issue of forgiveness had been settled. Although I never heard back from Bell, Mr. McAlister told me that Gene did read my letter, and he understood it.

How Far?

written by Dawn Smith Jordan, Phillip Sandifer and Kevin McAfee
Ephesians 4: 32 "Be kind and compassionate to one another, forgiving each other, just as in Christ, God forgave you."

To forgive
To forget
To release
To let go
These are words that I say,
But are they words that I mean
They've come from my heart,
But do I really know

Chorus:
How far must forgiveness go
How far must we go to know
Must we reach inside
Past the hurt to find
The grace shown through the ages
How far must forgiveness go

Past the hate
past the anger
Through His pain
Jesus cried
Tears of mercy, tears of love
And He forgave them as they took His life

Our selfless Savior has told us in one breath
Praying, "Father Forgive them."
He asked for those who caused His death

This is how far forgiveness must go
This is how far we must go to know
We must reach inside
Past the hurt to find
The grace shown through the ages
This is how far forgiveness must go

Performed by Dawn Smith Jordan, 1993 Urgent Music recording "How Far?" © 1993 243 Music/BMI, Urgent Music Group, P.O. Box 90754 Austin, TX 78709 (512) 282-4036

For me, life has moved on. In that hot month of June when I thought I was truly experiencing the heat of Hell, I could not see that any good would ever come of my life again. I wanted to quit and die. But God wouldn't let me. I thank God that my parents did not give up praying for me when I had strayed away from my commitment to the Lord. They asked Him every night to use my music for His glory. God honors those prayers, and I am reaping the blessings from them today.

Mom and Dad are on call with the Lexington Sheriff's Department twenty-four hours a day for parents who've lost children. Sometimes being able to take someone's hand and say, "I truly understand," to that hurting person is the greatest ministry of all. To them, I share a poem that was shared with me:

To All Parents

I'll lend you for a little time a child of Mine, He said,
For you to love the while he lives and mourn for when he's dead.
It may be six or seven years, or twenty-two or three,
But will you, till I call him back, take care of him for Me?
He'll bring his charms to gladden you, and shall his stay be brief
You'll have his lovely memories as solace for your grief.
I cannot promise he will stay since all from earth return,
But there are lessons taught down there I want this child to learn.
I've looked the wide world over in my search for teachers true
And from the throngs that crowd life's lanes I have selected you.
Now will you give him all your love, nor think the labor vain,
Nor hate Me when I come to call to take him back again?
I fancied that I hear them say: Dear Lord, Thy will be done
For all the joy Thy child shall bring the risk of grief we'll run.

We'll shelter him with tenderness; we'll love him while we may,
And for the happiness we've known, forever grateful stay;
But shall the angels call for him much sooner than we'd planned,
We'll have the bitter grief that comes and try to understand.

ANONYMOUS

Today my brother Robert is an honor graduate from Lees McRae College in Banner Elk, NC, where he attended on a basketball scholarship. He's not that skinny little boy anymore. He's grown into a fine young man, and I'm so very proud of him. I'm so grateful to God for the privilege of being his sister. When I was Miss South Carolina, I knew he got tired of being known as "Dawn Smith's little brother." Well, I want the world to know that I am proud to be Robert Smith's big sister! What a great blessing to my life he is.

Little did any of us realize what God could do in each of our lives. As Will and I continue together in our life and ministry, God's grace becomes even sweeter to us with each passing day. God has used the tragedy, Shari's testimony, and my family's testimony in ways we could not have imagined back in May of 1985. Our story appeared in the February 1989 issue of *Reader's Digest* and in countless other newspaper and magazine articles. Dear saints continue to tell me in all parts of our country, as I travel and minister, how they prayed for me and my family during that time. Humbly I thank them, knowing I will never be able to repay the debts I owe to so many whom God has used in my life.

Little did we know that during the same year God led me to write that difficult letter to my sister's murderer, a CBS made-for-television movie based on my family's story would touch the lives of countless millions across America and Canada with the incredible news of God's grace in the face of tragedy.

Shari is missed greatly, but her memory lives on in my mind and heart. The touch of her life on mine will never be erased. I still have the recurring dream that Shari comes back, alive, only to awaken hopeful, and then to feel the bitter sting of the truth in the darkness. To me, she will forever remain in my mind as a beautiful seventeen-year-old girl who loved life. Even as I sit here finishing the final pages of this book, it's hard to believe it's been seven years since I've seen her. Yet, Biblically, seven is a perfect number, and I can see how God's loving hand has brought gentle healing to me and my family, and is continuing to do so.

The tears still fall from my eyes when I'm missing her badly, missing the special relationship that sisters share, especially now as Will and I are expecting our first child. But I wouldn't want that for her. She's with her Father, the One who loves her so much more than I or my family even. Not one day passes that I don't think of her, remembering her with a smile. She was something else . . . and she still is.

It is my earnest prayer that you are going to be there when she and I see each other again after all this time. What a beautiful family reunion that will be! Sure, I want you to get to know Shari, but so much more than that, I want you to know my Jesus. He makes all the difference in the world.

Shari's testimony lives on in so many ways. I often find myself wondering what life would have been like if she had lived—especially at Christmas when our family gathers together. Would she be married . . . with children? Would we still be singing together . . . as the Smith Sisters? God allowed me the joy of having her as my sister for seventeen years, for which I will be eternally grateful. And I have the promise of having her as my sister for all eternity when I go to be with Jesus. I know that she's singing right now, just as she said, and I can hardly wait for the day when I can hear the song she's singing at Jesus' feet, more beautifully and perfectly than I have ever heard her, and I can join in. We will sing together again.

On those tough days of hectic schedules, tough days full of troubles and heartaches that come along in each of our lives, when I feel tempted in self-pity to say, "Okay, God, haven't I had enough of life's hardships? Couldn't you give me a break?" It's then that He gently re-reminds me in His still small voice that He gave me the biggest break He ever could when He sent His only Son to earth to die on a cruel cross for me. Jesus knows just how I feel when I hurt, when I'm angry, and when I'm just tired of it all. He suffered the greatest tragedy of all. He, too, was murdered—by my sin. Yet He tells me, even after all the weight of all the sin of all the world that He willingly bore, to come to Him with all of my burdens and weariness, and He'll give me rest.

Some who hear my story will still want to ask, "How in the world can you think God is a loving, merciful God after what you've been through?" After all He's brought me through, how can I think anything else of Him? What an incredible privilege it is to live for the God of the universe. But I have an even greater privilege—He lives in me! Just as an old song Shari and I used to sing together says, "If Heaven never was promised to me, it's been worth just having the Lord in my life." Even if He had never blessed my life in a way I could see or answered my prayers as I would like, He has done more than I could ever expect from a holy God. Only because of Him in my life have I found victory in the midst of my tragedy. Only in Him have I found joy in the midst of my sorrow and a peace that I cannot understand or explain. He is my All in All. Even back in those long, dark days of grief, when I wondered where God was, He was there.

Footprints

One night a man had a dream. He dreamed he was walking along the beach with the Lord. Across the sky flashed scenes from his life. For each scene, he noticed two sets of footprints in the sand; one belonged to him and the other to the Lord. When the last scene of his life flashed before him, he looked back at the footprints in the sand. He noticed that many times along the path of his life there was only one set of footprints. He also noticed that it happened at the very lowest and saddest times in his life.

This really bothered him, and he questioned the Lord about it. "Lord, You said that once I decided to follow You, You'd walk with me all the way. But I have noticed that during the most troublesome times in my life, there is only one set of footprints. I don't understand why when I needed You most, You would leave me."

The Lord replied, "My son, my precious child, I love you and I would never leave you. During your times of trial and suffering, when you see only one set of footprints, it was then that I carried you."

MARGARET FISHBACK POWERS

And He carried me too. God's grace. Marvelous grace.

Infinite grace. Matchless grace. Grace that is greater than all our sin and truly sufficient for me and for you. It truly is amazing grace. For every loved one lost, for every broken heart, every shattered life, for every single tragedy, for every disappointment and heartache, for every valley that seems to have no nearby mountaintop, for everyone who has ever asked why, and for every single pain, grief, and hurt that this world has to offer, God's grace is in the midst of it all. Where would I be without His gift of grace in my life? I praise Him that I don't even have to ask.

Amazing grace, how sweet the sound
that saved a wretch like me!
I once was lost, but now am found,
was blind, but now I see!

'Twas grace that taught my heart to fear,
and grace my fears relieved.
How precious did that grace appear
the hour I first believed.

Through many dangers, toils and snares
I have already come.
'Tis grace that brought me safe thus far,
and grace will lead me home!

When we've been there ten thousand years
bright shining as the sun!
We've no less days to sing God's praise
than when we've first begun!

For scheduling or product information, contact:
Jordan Ministries (803) 286-8331

Discography:
Taking a Stand, 1990, Renaissance Records
How Far?, 1993, Urgent Music Group
Canopy, 1995, Urgent Music Group
Available on cassette or compact disc

(Dawn Smith Jordan accompaniment tracks also available through Jordan Ministries)